Meatballs

pil

Publications International, Ltd.

Photography on pages 7, 15, 31, 43, 59, 71, 89, 105, 111, 115, 119 and 123 by PIL Photo Studio.
Photographer: Tate Hunt
Photographer's Assistant: Annemarie Zelasko
Prop Stylist: Tom Hamilton
Food Stylists: Kathy Joy, Carol Smoler
Assistant Food Stylists: Lisa Lecat-Knych, Lissa Levy

Pictured on the front cover: Turkey Meatballs in Cranberry-Barbecue Sauce *(page 4).*
Pictured on the back cover *(left to right):* Super Meatball Sliders *(page 30)* and Good Stuff Meatballs *(page 122).*

ISBN-13: 978-1-4508-2194-0
ISBN-10: 1-4508-2194-4

Library of Congress Control Number: 2011923515

Manufactured in China.

8 7 6 5 4 3 2 1

Microwave Cooking: Microwave ovens vary in wattage. Use the cooking times as guidelines and check for doneness before adding more time.

Preparation/Cooking Times: Preparation times are based on the approximate amount of time required to assemble the recipe before cooking, baking, chilling or serving. These times include preparation steps such as measuring, chopping and mixing. The fact that some preparations and cooking can be done simultaneously is taken into account. Preparation of optional ingredients and serving suggestions is not included.

Publications International, Ltd.

Contents

Party Pleasers

Turkey Meatballs in Cranberry-Barbecue Sauce

1 can (16 ounces) jellied cranberry sauce
½ cup barbecue sauce
1 egg white
1 pound ground turkey
1 green onion, sliced
2 teaspoons grated orange peel
1 teaspoon reduced-sodium soy sauce
¼ teaspoon black pepper
⅛ teaspoon ground red pepper (optional)

Slow Cooker Directions

1. Combine cranberry sauce and barbecue sauce in slow cooker. Cover; cook on HIGH 20 to 30 minutes or until cranberry sauce is melted.

2. Meanwhile, beat egg white in medium bowl. Add turkey, green onion, orange peel, soy sauce, black pepper and red pepper, if desired; mix well. Shape mixture into 24 meatballs.

3. Spray large nonstick skillet with cooking spray; heat over medium heat. Add meatballs; cook 8 to 10 minutes or until browned on all sides. Add to slow cooker; stir gently to coat with sauce.

4. *Turn slow cooker to LOW.* Cover; cook 3 hours.

Makes 12 servings

Sweet & Sour Meatballs

Meatballs
   1 pound lean ground pork, beef or turkey
   1 can (8 ounces) water chestnuts, drained and finely chopped
   1 egg
   ⅓ cup dry bread crumbs
   ½ teaspoon salt
Sauce
   ¼ cup finely chopped green onions
   1 tablespoon corn oil
   ¾ cup KARO® Light or Dark Corn Syrup
   ⅔ cup beef broth
   ½ cup chili sauce
   1 tablespoon cider vinegar
   1 teaspoon SPICE ISLANDS® Ground Ginger

1. For meatballs: Mix meat, water chestnuts, egg, bread crumbs and salt in medium bowl. Shape into 1-inch meatballs; set aside.

2. For sauce: Cook green onions in oil in large skillet, stirring frequently, for 1 to 2 minutes. Blend in corn syrup, broth, chili sauce, vinegar and ginger. Add meatballs; bring to boil. Reduce heat to medium.

3. Simmer 15 minutes. Remove meatballs with slotted spoon. Increase heat to medium-high; gently boil sauce 6 to 9 minutes or until thickened.

4. Pour sauce over meatballs. Serve with cocktail picks.

Makes 30 mini meatballs

Prep Time: 25 minutes • **Cook Time:** 25 minutes

Sweet & Sour Meatballs

Maple-Glazed Meatballs

1½ cups ketchup
1 cup maple syrup
⅓ cup reduced-sodium soy sauce
1 tablespoon quick-cooking tapioca
1½ teaspoons ground allspice
1 teaspoon dry mustard
2 packages (about 1 pound each) frozen fully cooked meatballs, partially thawed and separated
1 can (20 ounces) pineapple chunks in juice, drained

Slow Cooker Directions

1. Combine ketchup, maple syrup, soy sauce, tapioca, allspice and mustard in slow cooker.

2. Carefully stir meatballs and pineapple into ketchup mixture.

3. Cover; cook on LOW 5 to 6 hours. Stir before serving.

Makes about 4 dozen meatballs

Mini Turkey Meatballs Marinara

1 pound ground turkey
½ cup PEPPERIDGE FARM® Herb Seasoned Stuffing, crushed
½ cup grated Parmesan cheese
1 egg, beaten
Vegetable cooking spray
2¾ cups PREGO® Marinara Italian Sauce

1. Thoroughly mix the turkey, stuffing, cheese and egg in a large bowl. Shape the mixture into **42** (¾-inch) meatballs.

2. Spray a 12-inch nonstick skillet with cooking spray and heat over medium-high heat for 1 minute. Add the meatballs and cook in 2 batches or until they're well browned. Remove the meatballs with a slotted spoon and set aside.

3. Stir the sauce into the skillet. Heat to a boil. Return the meatballs to the skillet and reduce the heat to low. Cover and cook for 5 minutes or until the meatballs are cooked through. *Makes 42 meatballs*

Maple-Glazed Meatballs

Mexi-Meatball Kabobs

Nonstick cooking spray
3 pounds lean ground beef
2 cups quick oats
1 can (12 fluid ounces) NESTLÉ® CARNATION® Evaporated Milk
2 large eggs
½ cup ketchup
2 packets (1¼ ounces *each*) taco seasoning mix
1 teaspoon ground black pepper
3 large bell peppers (any color), cut into 60 (1-inch) pieces
60 4-inch wooden skewers
Salsa and sour cream (optional)

PREHEAT oven to 350°F. Foil-line 3 baking sheets and spray with nonstick cooking spray.

COMBINE ground beef, oats, evaporated milk, eggs, ketchup, taco seasoning and black pepper in large bowl until just mixed. Form mixture into 120 (1-inch) meatballs. Place on prepared baking sheets.

BAKE for 15 to 20 minutes or until no longer pink in center. Drain on paper towels, if needed.

THREAD two meatballs and one piece of pepper on *each* skewer. Place on large serving platter. Serve with salsa and sour cream.

Makes 30 servings (2 skewers each)

Tip: Meatballs can be made and baked ahead of time, refrigerated for up to 3 days or frozen up to 3 months and heated prior to serving.

Tip: Meatballs can also be served individually with toothpicks and dipping bowls of salsas.

Prep Time: 35 minutes • **Cook Time:** 15 minutes

Party Pleasers

Mexi-Meatball Kabobs

Barbecued Meatballs

2 pounds ground beef
1⅓ cups ketchup, divided
1 egg, beaten
3 tablespoons seasoned dry bread crumbs
2 tablespoons dried onion flakes
¾ teaspoon garlic salt
½ teaspoon black pepper
1 cup packed light brown sugar
1 can (6 ounces) tomato paste
¼ cup reduced-sodium soy sauce
¼ cup cider vinegar
1½ teaspoons hot pepper sauce
Diced bell peppers (optional)

Slow Cooker Directions

1. Preheat oven to 350°F. Combine beef, ⅓ cup ketchup, egg, bread crumbs, onion flakes, garlic salt and black pepper in large bowl; mix well. Shape mixture into 48 (1-inch) meatballs.

2. Place meatballs in single layer on two 15×10-inch jelly-roll pans. Bake 18 minutes or until browned. Transfer meatballs to slow cooker.

3. Mix remaining 1 cup ketchup, brown sugar, tomato paste, soy sauce, vinegar and hot pepper sauce in medium bowl. Pour over meatballs. Cover; cook on LOW 4 hours. Serve with cocktail picks. Garnish with bell peppers, if desired. *Makes 4 dozen meatballs*

Barbecued Franks: Place two (12-ounce) packages cocktail franks in slow cooker. Combine 1 cup ketchup with brown sugar, tomato paste, soy sauce, vinegar and hot pepper sauce in medium bowl; pour over franks. Cover; cook on LOW 4 hours.

Barbecued Meatballs

Savory Appetizer Pork Meatballs

1 pound ground pork
½ cup soft bread crumbs
1 egg, beaten
2 tablespoons minced onion
1 tablespoon minced green bell pepper
1 clove garlic, minced
1 teaspoon salt
⅛ teaspoon black pepper
1 tablespoon vegetable oil
1 can (8 ounces) tomato sauce
¼ cup apple jelly
¼ teaspoon curry powder

In large bowl combine ground pork, bread crumbs, egg, onion, bell pepper, garlic, salt and black pepper; mix well. Shape pork mixture into about 30 (1-inch) meatballs. In large skillet brown meatballs in hot oil. Drain well.

In small saucepan combine tomato sauce, apple jelly and curry powder; simmer until jelly is melted, stirring occasionally. Pour sauce over meatballs. Cover and simmer 15 to 20 minutes or until no longer pink in center, stirring often. *Makes 4 servings*

Prep Time: 20 minutes • **Cook Time:** 15 minutes

Favorite recipe from **National Pork Board**

Savory Appetizer Pork Meatballs

Easy Party Meatballs

3 cups (1 pound 10 ounces) PREGO® Marinara Italian Sauce
1 jar (12 ounces) grape jelly
½ cup prepared chili sauce
2½ pounds frozen fully-cooked meatballs, cocktail size

Slow Cooker Directions

1. Stir the Italian sauce, jelly, chili sauce and meatballs in a 4½-quart slow cooker.

2. Cover and cook on LOW for 6 to 7 hours* or until the meatballs are cooked through. Serve the meatballs on a serving plate with toothpicks.

Makes 8 servings

Or on HIGH for 3 to 4 hours.

Kitchen Tips: Larger-size or turkey meatballs can also be used, if desired. For a special touch, serve with cranberry chutney for dipping.

Mini Italian Meatballs

1 pound lean ground beef
¼ cup finely diced onion
3 teaspoons HERB-OX® beef flavored bouillon
½ cup Italian-style seasoned bread crumbs
1 egg, slightly beaten
¼ cup pizza sauce
   Vegetable oil, for frying
1 (10¾-ounce) can Italian herb tomato soup, undiluted
1 cup shredded mozzarella cheese

In bowl, combine ground beef, onion, bouillon, bread crumbs, egg and pizza sauce. Shape meat mixture in 48 (½-inch) meatballs. In large skillet, in a small amount of oil, cook meatballs until lightly browned on all sides. Place meatballs in a single layer in a 13×9-inch baking dish. Spoon soup over meatballs and sprinkle with cheese. Cover and bake at 350°F for 20 to 30 minutes or until meat is cooked through.

Makes 48 meatballs

Meatball Making: For 48 meatballs of equal size, shape meat mixture into an 8×6-inch rectangle on waxed paper. Cut into 1-inch squares; roll each square into a ball.

Easy Party Meatballs

Cocktail Meatballs

1 pound ground beef
1 pound bulk pork or Italian sausage
1 cup cracker crumbs
1 cup finely chopped onion
1 cup finely chopped green bell pepper
½ cup milk
1 egg, beaten
2 teaspoons salt
1 teaspoon Italian seasoning
¼ teaspoon black pepper
1 cup ketchup
¾ cup packed brown sugar
½ cup (1 stick) butter, cut into pieces
½ cup cider vinegar
¼ cup water
¼ cup lemon juice
1 teaspoon yellow mustard
¼ teaspoon garlic salt

Slow Cooker Directions

1. Preheat oven to 350°F. Combine beef, sausage, cracker crumbs, onion, bell pepper, milk, egg, salt, Italian seasoning and black pepper in large bowl; mix well. Shape mixture into 1-inch meatballs.

2. Place meatballs on racks on two nonstick baking sheets. Bake 25 minutes or until meatballs are browned.

3. Meanwhile, place ketchup, brown sugar, butter, vinegar, water, lemon juice, mustard and garlic salt in slow cooker; mix well. Cover; cook on HIGH 30 minutes.

4. Transfer meatballs to slow cooker; carefully stir to coat with sauce. *Turn slow cooker to LOW.* Cover; cook 2 hours.   *Makes 12 servings*

Cocktail Meatballs

Mini Meatballs with Red Pepper Dipping Sauce

1 bottled roasted red pepper, drained and coarsely chopped
2 cloves garlic, divided
¼ cup mayonnaise
⅛ teaspoon red pepper flakes (optional)
¼ pound ground beef
¼ pound ground pork
1 cup plain dry bread crumbs, divided
1 shallot, minced
¼ teaspoon salt
⅛ teaspoon black pepper
1 egg, beaten
¼ cup vegetable oil

1. For Red Pepper Dipping Sauce, place roasted red pepper and 1 clove garlic in blender; blend until smooth. Transfer to small bowl; stir in mayonnaise and red pepper flakes, if desired.

2. Mince remaining clove garlic. Combine beef, pork, ¼ cup bread crumbs, shallot, garlic, salt and black pepper in medium bowl. Add egg; mix well. Shape mixture into 32 to 36 (1-inch) meatballs.

3. Spread remaining ¾ cup bread crumbs on large plate. Roll meatballs in bread crumbs.

4. Heat oil in large skillet over medium-high heat. Add meatballs in batches; cook 8 minutes, turning frequently until browned on all sides and cooked through (160°F). Drain on paper towels. Serve with Red Pepper Dipping Sauce. *Makes about 8 servings*

Tip: Some supermarkets sell a meat loaf blend of half beef and half pork; use ½ pound of the blend. Or substitute all pork in this recipe.

Note: Red Pepper Dipping Sauce may be prepared and refrigerated up to 4 hours in advance. Allow the sauce to come to room temperature before serving.

Mini Meatballs with Red Pepper Dipping Sauce

Salsa Party Meatballs

2½ pounds ground beef or ground meat loaf mix (beef, pork and veal)
  6 tablespoons dry bread crumbs
¼ cup milk
  2 eggs
  1 teaspoon garlic powder
  4 green onions, chopped (about ½ cup)
  1 cup shredded Cheddar cheese (about 4 ounces)
  2 tablespoons olive or vegetable oil
  2 jars (16 ounces each) PACE® Picante Sauce

1. Mix the beef, bread crumbs, milk, eggs, garlic powder, green onions and **2 tablespoons** cheese thoroughly in a large bowl. Shape firmly into 30 (1½-inch) meatballs.

2. Heat the oil in a 12-inch nonstick skillet over medium-high heat. Add the meatballs and cook until they're well browned. Pour off any fat.

3. Stir the picante sauce in the skillet and heat to a boil. Reduce the heat to low. Cover and cook for 10 minutes or until the meatballs are cooked through. Stir in the remaining cheese and cook for 1 minute or until the cheese is melted. Sprinkle with additional chopped green onions, if desired. Serve with toothpicks.   *Makes 30 meatballs*

Prep Time: 5 minutes • **Cook Time:** 25 minutes • **Total Time:** 30 minutes

To make a ground meat mixture easier to handle,
dampen your hands with cold water before
shaping the mixture into meatballs.

Salsa Party Meatballs

Raspberry-Balsamic Glazed Meatballs

1 package (about 2 pounds) frozen fully cooked meatballs
1 cup raspberry preserves
3 tablespoons sugar
3 tablespoons balsamic vinegar
1 tablespoon plus 1½ teaspoons Worcestershire sauce
¼ teaspoon red pepper flakes
1 tablespoon grated fresh ginger (optional)

Slow Cooker Directions

1. Spray slow cooker with nonstick cooking spray. Add meatballs.

2. Combine preserves, sugar, vinegar, Worcestershire sauce and red pepper flakes in small microwavable bowl. Microwave on HIGH 45 seconds; stir. Microwave 15 seconds or until melted (mixture will be chunky). Reserve ½ cup preserves mixture. Pour remaining mixture over meatballs; stir to coat. Cover; cook on LOW 5 hours or on HIGH 2½ hours.

3. *Turn slow cooker to HIGH.* Stir in ginger, if desired, and reserved ½ cup preserves mixture. Cook, uncovered, 15 to 20 minutes or until thickened slightly, stirring occasionally.   *Makes about 32 meatballs*

Serving Suggestion: To serve as a main dish, toss with chopped green onions and serve over hot rice. Makes 8 main-dish servings.

25

Raspberry-Balsamic Glazed Meatballs

Mexican Meatballs

3 ORTEGA® Yellow Corn Taco Shells
1 pound lean ground beef
1 egg
2 teaspoons ORTEGA® Fire-Roasted Diced Green Chiles
1 teaspoon ORTEGA® Chili Seasoning Mix
1 bottle (8 ounces) ORTEGA® Taco Sauce
¼ cup (1 ounce) shredded Cheddar cheese
    Diced cilantro (optional)

Break taco shells into food processor and pulse several times to create about ½ cup taco shell crumbs. Place into large mixing bowl and add ground beef, egg, chiles and seasoning mix. Mix thoroughly.

Form mixture into 30 (1-inch) meatballs and drop into hot skillet. Cook meatballs until they begin to brown. Carefully turn meatballs over and continue browning. Add taco sauce. Coat meatballs with sauce and simmer over low heat, uncovered, 10 minutes.

Sprinkle meatballs with cheese and garnish with cilantro, if desired. Serve with toothpicks.   *Makes about 30 meatballs*

Note: For variety, replace the ground beef with either ground chicken or ground turkey.

Prep Time: 15 minutes • **Start to Finish Time:** 30 minutes

Mini Cocktail Meatballs

1 envelope LIPTON® RECIPE SECRETS® Onion, Onion Mushroom
    or Beefy Onion Soup Mix
1 pound ground beef
½ cup plain dry bread crumbs
¼ cup dry red wine or water
2 eggs, lightly beaten

1. Preheat oven to 375°F.

2. In medium bowl, combine all ingredients; shape into 1-inch meatballs.

3. In shallow baking pan, arrange meatballs and bake 18 minutes or until done. Serve, if desired, with assorted mustards or tomato sauce.

Makes about 4 dozen meatballs

Party Pleasers

Mexican Meatballs

Turkey Meatballs with Sweet & Sour Sauce

1 pound ground turkey
½ cup seasoned dry bread crumbs
1 egg, slightly beaten
1 tablespoon dried onion flakes
1 tablespoon green bell pepper, chopped
2 tablespoons hoisin sauce
   Nonstick vegetable cooking spray
½ cup lightly packed brown sugar
2 tablespoons cornstarch
1 can (20 ounces) pineapple chunks, drained and juice reserved
⅓ cup water
3 tablespoons rice wine vinegar
1 tablespoon reduced sodium soy sauce
1 large red bell pepper, cut into ½-inch pieces

Preheat oven to 400°F. In medium bowl combine turkey, bread crumbs, egg, onion flakes, chopped green pepper and hoisin sauce. Mix well; cover and refrigerate for about 30 minutes or until mixture is well chilled. Shape 30 meatballs from turkey mixture (approximately 1 tablespoon for each meatball).

Coat 15×10×1-inch jelly-roll pan with nonstick cooking spray. Arrange meatballs in an even single layer on pan; bake 15 to 20 minutes or until meatballs are no longer pink in center.

Meanwhile, in 2-quart microwave-safe dish, combine brown sugar and cornstarch. Stir in reserved pineapple juice, water, vinegar and soy sauce. Microwave at HIGH (100% power) 2 minutes; stir in red pepper pieces. Microwave at HIGH 3 minutes, stirring halfway through cooking time. Fold in meatballs and pineapple chunks. Microwave at HIGH 2 minutes or until mixture is heated through. Transfer meatball mixture to chafing dish and serve with toothpicks. *Makes 15 servings*

Favorite recipe from **National Turkey Federation**

Pineapple Glazed
Cocktail Meatballs

1 can (about 20 ounces) pineapple chunks in heavy syrup
2 tablespoons cornstarch
1½ cups V8® 100% Vegetable Juice (Regular or Low Sodium)
1 pound ground beef
¼ cup dry bread crumbs
1 egg, beaten
1 teaspoon garlic powder
¼ teaspoon ground black pepper
1 tablespoon vegetable oil

1. Drain the pineapple, reserving the syrup. Stir the cornstarch, 1¼ cups vegetable juice and syrup in a small bowl until the mixture is smooth and set it aside.

2. Mix the remaining vegetable juice, beef, bread crumbs, egg, garlic powder and pepper thoroughly. Shape firmly into **24** (1-inch) meatballs.

3. Heat the oil in a 10-inch skillet over medium-high heat. Add the meatballs in 2 batches and cook until they're well browned on all sides. Set the meatballs aside. Pour off any fat.

4. Stir the cornstarch mixture and add it to the skillet. Heat to a boil, stirring constantly. Return the meatballs to the skillet. Add the pineapple chunks. Reduce the heat to low and cook for 5 minutes or until the mixture thickens and the meatballs are cooked through. *Makes 24 meatballs*

Prep Time: 20 minutes • **Cook Time:** 20 minutes • **Total Time:** 40 minutes

Family Favorites

Super Meatball Sliders

1 can (15 ounces) whole berry cranberry sauce
1 can (about 15 ounces) tomato sauce
1/8 teaspoon red pepper flakes (optional)
2 pounds ground beef or turkey
3/4 cup bread crumbs
1 egg, beaten
1 package onion soup mix
Baby arugula leaves
24 small potato rolls or dinner rolls
6 slices (1 ounce each) provolone cheese, cut into quarters

1. Preheat oven to 350°F. Combine cranberry sauce, tomato sauce and red pepper flakes, if desired, in medium bowl.

2. Combine beef, bread crumbs, egg and soup mix in large bowl; mix well. Shape mixture into 24 meatballs (about 1¾ inches). Place in 13×9-inch baking pan or glass baking dish; pour sauce over meatballs, making sure all meatballs are covered.

3. Bake 40 to 45 minutes or until meatballs are cooked through (160°F), basting with sauce once or twice.

4. Place arugula on rolls; top with meatballs and cheese. Spoon sauce from pan over meatballs. *Makes 2 dozen sliders*

Vegetable Spaghetti Sauce with Meatballs

1½ cups sliced fresh mushrooms
½ cup chopped onion
½ cup chopped carrot
½ cup chopped green bell pepper
2 cloves garlic, minced
2 cans (about 14 ounces each) stewed tomatoes, undrained
1 can (6 ounces) tomato paste
2½ teaspoons Italian seasoning, divided
½ teaspoon salt
¼ teaspoon black pepper
1 egg white, beaten
2 tablespoons fine dry bread crumbs
2 tablespoons finely chopped onion
½ pound ground beef
4 cups hot cooked spaghetti

1. Spray large saucepan with nonstick cooking spray; heat over medium heat. Add mushrooms, ½ cup onion, carrot, bell pepper and garlic; cook and stir 4 to 5 minutes or until vegetables are crisp-tender. Stir in stewed tomatoes with juice, tomato paste, 2 teaspoons Italian seasoning, salt and black pepper; bring to a boil over medium-high heat. Reduce heat to medium-low; cover and simmer 20 minutes, stirring occasionally.

2. Preheat oven to 375°F. Combine egg white, bread crumbs, 2 tablespoons onion and remaining ½ teaspoon Italian seasoning in medium bowl. Add beef; mix well. Shape mixture into 16 meatballs. Place in 11×7-inch baking pan. Bake 18 to 20 minutes or until cooked through (160°F). Drain on paper towels.

3. Stir meatballs into sauce; return to a boil. Simmer, uncovered, over medium-low heat about 10 minutes or until sauce thickens slightly, stirring occasionally. Serve over spaghetti. *Makes 4 servings*

Vegetable Spaghetti Sauce with Meatballs

Fusilli Pizzaiola with Turkey Meatballs

1 pound ground turkey
1 egg, beaten
1 tablespoon milk
¼ cup Italian seasoned dry bread crumbs
2 tablespoons chopped fresh parsley
¼ teaspoon black pepper, divided
½ cup chopped onion
½ cup grated carrot
1 clove garlic, minced
2 teaspoons olive oil
2 cans (about 14 ounces each) diced tomatoes
2 tablespoons chopped fresh basil *or* 2 teaspoons dried basil
1 tablespoon tomato paste
½ teaspoon dried thyme
1 bay leaf
8 ounces uncooked fusilli or other spiral-shaped pasta

1. Preheat oven to 350°F. Spray baking sheet with nonstick cooking spray.

2. Combine turkey, egg and milk in medium bowl. Add bread crumbs, parsley and ⅛ teaspoon pepper; mix well. Shape mixture into 24 (1-inch) meatballs with wet hands. Place meatballs on baking sheet. Bake 25 minutes or until cooked through (165°F).

3. Place onion, carrot, garlic and oil in medium saucepan; cook and stir over high heat 5 minutes or until onion is tender. Add tomatoes, basil, tomato paste, thyme, bay leaf and remaining ⅛ teaspoon pepper; bring to a boil. Reduce heat to low; simmer 25 minutes. Add meatballs; cover and simmer 5 to 10 minutes or until sauce thickens slightly. Remove and discard bay leaf.

4. Meanwhile, cook pasta according to package directions; drain. Spoon meatballs and sauce over pasta. *Makes 4 servings*

Fusilli Pizzaiola with Turkey Meatballs

Mafalda and Meatballs

1 teaspoon olive oil
2 cloves garlic, minced, divided
2 cans (about 14 ounces each) stewed tomatoes, undrained
½ teaspoon dried basil
½ pound ground beef
½ pound ground turkey
⅓ cup plain dry bread crumbs
3 tablespoons reduced-sodium chicken broth
1 egg, beaten
1 teaspoon whole fennel seeds
¼ teaspoon salt
⅛ teaspoon black pepper
8 ounces uncooked mafalda pasta or spaghetti
Grated Parmesan cheese (optional)

1. Heat oil in large nonstick saucepan over medium-high heat. Add half of garlic; cook and stir 1 minute. Add tomatoes with juice and basil; bring to a boil. Reduce heat to low; simmer 20 to 25 minutes or until sauce thickens, stirring occasionally.

2. Meanwhile, combine beef, turkey, bread crumbs, broth, egg, fennel seeds, remaining half of garlic, salt and pepper in large bowl; mix well. Shape mixture into 12 (1-inch) meatballs with wet hands.

3. Preheat broiler. Spray broiler pan with nonstick cooking spray. Place meatballs on broiler pan. Broil 4 inches from heat 10 minutes or until cooked through (165°F). Add meatballs to sauce; cover and cook 5 to 10 minutes or until heated through.

4. Cook pasta according to package directions; drain. Place pasta on serving platter; top with meatballs and sauce. Serve with cheese, if desired. *Makes 4 servings*

Devilishly Divine Creamy Tomato Sauce with Meatballs

2 pounds turkey sausage, uncooked, casings removed
1 cup plain dry bread crumbs
2 jars (26 ounces *each*) prepared marinara sauce
1 can (12 ounces) NESTLÉ® CARNATION® Evaporated Milk
¾ teaspoon red pepper flakes
1 pound dry spaghetti or pasta of your choice, cooked and kept warm
  Chopped fresh parsley (optional)

PREHEAT oven to 350°F. Line baking sheet with sides with foil.

COMBINE sausage and bread crumbs in large bowl. Form mixture into 60 (1-inch) meatballs. Place on prepared baking sheet.

BAKE for 15 minutes or until no longer pink. Drain meatballs on paper towel-lined plates.

MEANWHILE, combine marinara sauce, evaporated milk and red pepper flakes in large saucepan. Cook over medium heat, stirring occasionally, for 10 minutes or until simmering. Add meatballs; stir.

SERVE *half* the sauce and meatballs over cooked spaghetti. Top with parsley, if desired.   *Makes 12 servings*

Tip: Freeze the remaining sauce and meatballs for another meal. Thaw in refrigerator and reheat in microwave or on stovetop. Serve with pasta of your choice.

Prep Time: 15 minutes • **Cook Time:** 20 minutes

Mama's Best Ever
Spaghetti & Meatballs

1 pound lean ground beef
½ cup Italian seasoned dry bread crumbs
1 egg
1 jar (1 pound 10 ounces) RAGÚ® Old World Style® Pasta Sauce
8 ounces spaghetti, cooked and drained

1. Combine ground beef, bread crumbs and egg in medium bowl; shape into 12 meatballs.

2. Bring Pasta Sauce to a boil over medium-high heat in 3-quart saucepan. Gently stir in uncooked meatballs. Reduce heat to low and simmer covered, stirring occasionally, 20 minutes or until meatballs are done.

3. Serve over hot spaghetti and garnish, if desired, with grated Parmesan cheese. *Makes 4 servings*

Kid's Choice Meatballs

1½ pounds ground beef
¼ cup seasoned dry bread crumbs
¼ cup grated Parmesan cheese
3 tablespoons FRENCH'S® Worcestershire Sauce
1 egg
2 jars (14 ounces each) spaghetti sauce

1. Preheat oven to 425°F. In bowl, gently mix beef, bread crumbs, cheese, Worcestershire and egg. Shape into 1-inch meatballs. Place on rack in roasting pan. Bake 15 minutes or until cooked.

2. In large saucepan, combine meatballs and spaghetti sauce. Cook until heated through. Serve over cooked pasta.
Makes 6 to 8 servings (about 48 meatballs)

Quick Meatball Tip: On waxed paper, pat meat mixture into 8×6×1-inch rectangle. With knife, cut crosswise and lengthwise into 1-inch rows. Roll each small square into a ball.

Prep Time: 10 minutes • **Cook Time:** 20 minutes

Mama's Best Ever Spaghetti & Meatballs

Baked Turkey Meatballs

½ cup steel-cut or old-fashioned oats
1 egg white, beaten
1 pound ground turkey
1 clove garlic, minced
½ teaspoon salt
¼ to ½ teaspoon black pepper
⅛ teaspoon nutmeg
1 medium zucchini, shredded (about 1 cup)
2 cups marinara sauce
3 cups cooked spaghetti

1. Preheat oven to 400°F. Spray broiling or baking pan with nonstick cooking spray.

2. Mix oats and egg white in small bowl. Combine turkey, garlic, salt, pepper and nutmeg in medium bowl. Add zucchini and oat mixture; mix well.

3. Shape mixture into 24 meatballs. Place on prepared pan. Bake 12 to 15 minutes.

4. Place meatballs and marinara sauce in medium saucepan; bring to a boil over medium-high heat. Reduce heat to medium-low; simmer about 10 minutes. Serve over spaghetti.   *Makes 6 servings*

Use regular ground turkey (85% lean), a combination of white and dark meat, for meatballs. Ground turkey breast is very low in fat (up to 99% lean) and can dry out easily.

Baked Turkey Meatballs

Rigatoni with Sausage Meatballs

½ pound bulk mild Italian sausage
½ pound ground beef
 1 onion, chopped
 1 can (about 14 ounces) diced tomatoes
 1 can (6 ounces) tomato paste
½ teaspoon dried oregano
¼ teaspoon salt
 8 ounces uncooked rigatoni or cavatappi pasta
⅓ cup grated Parmesan cheese

1. Shape sausage into ½-inch meatballs. Brown meatballs in large skillet over medium-high heat 3 minutes, stirring frequently. Remove from skillet.

2. Add beef and onion to skillet; cook until no longer pink, stirring to break up meat. Drain fat. Stir in meatballs, tomatoes, tomato paste, oregano and salt; simmer 10 minutes over medium-low heat.

3. Meanwhile, cook pasta according to package directions; drain. Stir pasta into sauce. Sprinkle with cheese. *Makes 4 servings*

Savory Meatballs & Sauce

 2 pounds ground beef
 1 envelope LIPTON® RECIPE SECRETS® Onion Soup Mix
½ cup plain dry bread crumbs
 1 jar (45 ounces) RAGÚ® Old World Style® Pasta Sauce, divided
 1 tablespoon BERTOLLI® Olive Oil
 1 pound spaghetti, cooked and drained

1. In large bowl, combine ground beef, soup mix, bread crumbs and ½ cup Pasta Sauce. Shape into 16 (2-inch) balls.

2. In large saucepan, heat olive oil over medium-high heat and cook ½ of the meatballs 6 minutes, turning once. Remove and set aside. Repeat with remaining meatballs.

3. Return meatballs to saucepan; add remaining Pasta Sauce. Gently stir to cover meatballs. Bring to a boil. Reduce heat to low and simmer covered, 25 minutes or until meatballs are done. Serve over hot cooked spaghetti. *Makes 4 servings*

Rigatoni with Sausage Meatballs

Scotto Sunday Sauce
with Meatballs

½ cup olive oil
3 large onions, diced (about 3 cups)
2 tablespoons minced garlic
6 cups PREGO® Flavored with Meat Italian Sauce
4 fresh basil leaves, chopped
1 teaspoon crushed red pepper
6 slices thawed PEPPERIDGE FARM® Garlic Texas Toast, diced
½ cup whole milk
1½ pounds ground beef
2 eggs
¼ cup grated Parmesan cheese

1. Heat ¼ cup oil in a 6-quart saucepot over medium heat. Add **2 cups** onions and the garlic and cook until the onion is tender. Stir the Italian sauce, basil and red pepper in the saucepot. Remove the saucepot from the heat.

2. Place the bread into a large bowl. Pour the milk over the bread. Stir and press the bread into the milk to coat. Let stand for 5 minutes.

3. Add the beef, remaining onions, eggs and cheese to the bread mixture. Mix the beef mixture thoroughly and shape firmly into **12** (3-inch) meatballs. Place the meatballs onto a baking sheet. Cover and refrigerate for 15 minutes.

4. Heat the remaining oil in a 12-inch skillet over medium-high heat. Add the meatballs in batches and cook until they're well browned.

5. Add the meatballs to the sauce mixture. Cook over medium heat for 15 minutes or until the meatballs are cooked through. Serve with additional Texas toast or garlic bread, if desired.   *Makes 6 servings*

Quick Meatballs in Tomato Sauce

1 pound lean ground beef
¼ cup CREAM OF WHEAT® Hot Cereal (Instant, 1-minute, 2½-minute
     or 10-minute cook time), uncooked
¼ cup grated Parmesan cheese
¼ cup milk
¼ cup minced fresh parsley
1 egg
½ teaspoon ground black pepper
¼ teaspoon garlic salt
2 tablespoons olive oil
2 tablespoons POLANER® Chopped Garlic
1 (28-ounce) can crushed tomatoes
½ cup water
    Cooked pasta (optional)
    Grated Parmesan cheese for garnish
    Fresh chopped parsley (optional)

1. Mix ground beef, Cream of Wheat, cheese, milk, parsley, egg, pepper and garlic salt in large mixing bowl until well blended.

2. Heat oil in large skillet over medium-high heat. Add garlic; cook and stir 3 minutes or until lightly browned. Stir in crushed tomatoes and water.

3. Form beef mixture into 1-inch balls. Add to skillet; cover. Cook over medium-high heat 10 minutes.

4. Turn meatballs over to cover with sauce. Simmer over low heat 5 minutes longer. Serve over pasta, if desired. Garnish with cheese and parsley, if desired. *Makes 4 servings*

Tip: This recipe makes 20 to 24 meatballs, so you can also serve them as a great game-day snack. Just provide toothpicks so family and friends can help themselves to this tasty appetizer.

Prep Time: 10 minutes • **Start to Finish Time:** 25 minutes

Spaghetti & Meatballs

8 ounces uncooked multigrain or whole wheat spaghetti
¾ pound ground beef
¼ pound hot turkey Italian sausage, casing removed
1 egg white, beaten
2 tablespoons plain dry bread crumbs
1 teaspoon dried oregano
2 cups tomato-basil pasta sauce
3 tablespoons chopped fresh basil
¼ cup grated Parmesan cheese

1. Preheat oven to 450°F. Spray baking sheet with nonstick cooking spray. Cook spaghetti according to package directions; drain.

2. Combine beef, sausage, egg white, bread crumbs and oregano in medium bowl; mix well. Shape mixture into 16 (1½-inch) meatballs. Place on prepared baking sheet. Bake 12 minutes, turning once.

3. Pour pasta sauce into large skillet; add meatballs. Cook and stir over medium heat 9 minutes or until meatballs are cooked through (160°F).

4. Divide spaghetti among four plates. Top with meatballs and sauce; sprinkle with basil and cheese.   *Makes 4 servings*

If you don't have bread crumbs on hand, you can crush unsweetened cereal or crackers into crumbs to use as a substitute. (Use the same amount called for in the recipe.)

Family Favorites

Spaghetti & Meatballs

Hearty Meatball Stew

1 pound ground turkey breast or extra-lean ground beef
¾ cup QUAKER® Oats (quick or old fashioned, uncooked)
1 can (8 ounces) no-salt-added tomato sauce, divided
1½ teaspoons garlic powder
1½ teaspoons dried thyme leaves, divided
2 cans (14½ ounces each) reduced-sodium, fat-free chicken broth
¾ teaspoon salt (optional)
⅓ cup ditalini or other small pasta
2½ cups any frozen vegetable blend (do not thaw)
¼ cup water
2 tablespoons cornstarch

1. Heat broiler. Lightly spray rack of broiler pan with nonstick cooking spray.

2. Combine turkey, oats, ⅓ cup tomato sauce, garlic powder and 1 teaspoon thyme in large bowl; mix lightly but thoroughly. Transfer to sheet of aluminum foil or waxed paper. Pat mixture into 9×6-inch rectangle. Cut into 1½-inch squares; roll each square into a ball. Arrange meatballs on broiler pan.

3. Broil meatballs 6 to 8 inches from heat about 6 minutes or until cooked through, turning once.

4. While meatballs cook, bring broth, remaining tomato sauce, remaining ½ teaspoon thyme and salt, if desired, to a boil in 4-quart saucepan or Dutch oven over medium-high heat. Add pasta and vegetables; return to a boil. Reduce heat, cover and simmer 10 minutes or until pasta and vegetables are tender. Stir together water and cornstarch in small bowl until smooth. Add to saucepan along with meatballs. Cook and stir until broth is thickened. Spoon into bowls. *Makes 6 servings*

Hearty Meatball Stew

Cheesy Stuffed Meatballs & Spaghetti

1 pound ground beef
½ cup Italian seasoned dry bread crumbs
1 egg
2 ounces mozzarella cheese, cut into 12 (½-inch) cubes
1 jar (1 pound 10 ounces) RAGÚ® Old World Style® Pasta Sauce
8 ounces spaghetti, cooked and drained

1. In medium bowl, combine ground beef, bread crumbs and egg; shape into 12 meatballs. Press 1 cheese cube into each meatball, enclosing completely.

2. In 3-quart saucepan, bring Pasta Sauce to a boil over medium-high heat. Gently stir in uncooked meatballs.

3. Reduce heat to low and simmer covered, stirring occasionally, 20 minutes or until meatballs are done. Serve over hot spaghetti. Sprinkle, if desired, with grated Parmesan cheese.   *Makes 4 servings*

Prep Time: 20 minutes • **Cook Time:** 20 minutes

Quick Meatball Stroganoff

24 prepared frozen meatballs, thawed (about 12 ounces)
1 can (10¾ ounces) condensed cream of chicken soup
1 tablespoon FRENCH'S® Worcestershire Sauce
1 container (8 ounces) sour cream
1 cup FRENCH'S® French Fried Onions
   Hot cooked noodles

1. In large saucepan, combine meatballs, soup, Worcestershire and ½ cup water.

2. Bring to boiling. Reduce heat. Cover; simmer 10 to 15 minutes or until meatballs are heated through.

3. Stir in sour cream. Serve over noodles. Sprinkle with French Fried Onions. Sprinkle with paprika or minced parsley, if desired.
                                        Makes 4 to 6 servings

Prep Time: 5 minutes • **Cook Time:** 10 minutes

Family Favorites

Cheesy Stuffed Meatballs & Spaghetti

Classic Italian Meatballs

1½ pounds meat loaf mix* or lean ground beef
⅓ cup plain dry bread crumbs
⅓ cup grated onion
⅓ cup milk
¼ cup grated Parmesan cheese
1 egg, beaten
2 cloves garlic, minced
1½ teaspoons dried basil
1 teaspoon salt
1 teaspoon dried oregano
½ teaspoon dried sage
¼ teaspoon red pepper flakes
3 to 4 cups marinara sauce
Hot cooked pasta
Additional grated Parmesan cheese (optional)

Meat loaf mix is a combination of ground beef, pork and veal; it can be found in some supermarkets. You can make your own mix with 1 pound lean ground beef, ¼ pound ground pork and ¼ pound ground veal.

1. Preheat oven to 400°F. Spray broiler pan with nonstick cooking spray.

2. Combine meat loaf mix, bread crumbs, onion, milk, ¼ cup cheese, egg, garlic, basil, salt, oregano, sage and red pepper flakes in large bowl; mix well. Shape mixture into meatballs using ⅓ cup mixture for each. Place in prepared pan; bake 30 minutes.

3. Bring marinara sauce to a simmer in large saucepan over medium heat. Add meatballs; simmer over low heat about 10 minutes or until meatballs are cooked through (160°F.)

4. Serve meatballs over pasta; top with sauce. Serve with additional cheese, if desired.   *Makes 4 to 6 servings*

Family Favorites

Classic Italian Meatballs

Porcupine Meatballs

1 pound ground turkey
2 cups cooked regular brown rice or regular long-grain white rice
1 egg
¾ teaspoon dried oregano leaves, crushed
½ teaspoon garlic powder
¼ teaspoon ground black pepper
1 jar (24 ounces) PREGO® Traditional or Tomato, Basil & Garlic Italian Sauce

1. Mix the turkey, rice, egg, oregano, garlic powder and black pepper thoroughly in a medium bowl and shape firmly into **25** meatballs.

2. Heat the Italian sauce in a 12-inch skillet over medium heat. Add the meatballs and heat to a boil. Reduce the heat to low. Cover and cook for 10 minutes or until the meatballs are cooked through.

Makes 5 servings

Meatballs with Parsley and BelGioioso® Parmesan

4 large eggs
½ cup fresh bread crumbs
6 tablespoons grated BELGIOIOSO® Parmesan Cheese
¼ cup chopped fresh parsley
3 tablespoons olive oil
3 large cloves garlic, minced
2 teaspoons salt
1 teaspoon ground black pepper
2 pounds lean ground beef
Additional olive oil (for frying)

Combine eggs, bread crumbs, BelGioioso Parmesan Cheese, parsley, 3 tablespoons olive oil, garlic, salt and pepper in large bowl. Add ground beef and mix thoroughly. Form mixture into 1½-inch balls.

Pour enough oil into heavy large skillet to coat bottom; heat over medium-low heat. Working in batches, add meatballs. Cook until brown and cooked through, turning frequently, about 15 minutes per batch. Add more oil as needed. Transfer to plate and serve. *Makes 8 servings*

Porcupine Meatballs

Baked Italian Meatballs

1 pound ground beef (90% to 95% lean)
¼ cup seasoned dry bread crumbs
1 egg
2 tablespoons water
1 teaspoon minced garlic
½ teaspoon salt
⅛ teaspoon black pepper
1 jar (14½ ounces) pasta sauce, heated
Hot cooked pasta or crusty Italian rolls (optional)

1. Heat oven to 400°F. Combine ground beef, bread crumbs, egg, water, garlic, salt and pepper in large bowl, mixing lightly but thoroughly. Shape into 12 two-inch meatballs. Place on rack in broiler pan. Bake in 400°F oven 17 to 19 minutes.

2. Serve with pasta sauce over hot cooked pasta or as sandwiches in crusty Italian rolls, if desired. *Makes 4 servings*

Cook's Tip: Cooking times are for fresh or thoroughly thawed ground beef. Ground beef should be cooked to an internal temperature of 160°F. Color is not a reliable indicator of ground beef doneness.

Prep and Cook Time: 30 to 35 minutes

Favorite recipe from **Courtesy The Beef Checkoff**

Baked Italian Meatballs

Bowls & Rolls

Acorn Squash Soup with Chicken and Red Pepper Meatballs

  1 small to medium acorn squash (about ¾ pound)
½ pound ground chicken or turkey
  1 red bell pepper, seeded and finely chopped
  3 tablespoons egg substitute
  1 teaspoon dried parsley
  1 teaspoon ground coriander
½ teaspoon black pepper
¼ teaspoon ground cinnamon
  3 cups reduced-sodium vegetable broth
  2 tablespoons sour cream (optional)
    Ground red pepper (optional)

1. Pierce squash skin with fork. Place in microwavable dish; microwave on HIGH 8 to 10 minutes or until tender. Cool 10 minutes.

2. Meanwhile, combine chicken, bell pepper, egg substitute, parsley, coriander, black pepper and cinnamon in large bowl; mix well. Shape mixture into 8 meatballs. Place meatballs in microwavable dish; microwave on HIGH 5 minutes or until cooked through (165°F).

3. Remove and discard seeds from cooled squash. Scrape flesh from shell into large saucepan; mash squash with potato masher. Add broth and meatballs to saucepan; cook over medium-high heat 12 minutes, stirring occasionally. Add additional broth, if necessary, to thin soup.

4. Garnish each serving with sour cream and ground red pepper.

Makes 2 servings

Italian Meatball Subs

½ cup chopped onion
3 teaspoons finely chopped garlic, divided
1 can (about 14 ounces) Italian-style crushed tomatoes, undrained
2 bay leaves
2½ teaspoons dried basil, divided
2 teaspoons dried oregano, divided
¾ teaspoon black pepper, divided
¼ teaspoon red pepper flakes
½ pound ground beef
⅓ cup chopped green onions
⅓ cup plain dry bread crumbs
¼ cup chopped fresh parsley
1 egg white, beaten
2 tablespoons water
½ teaspoon dried marjoram
½ teaspoon ground mustard
4 French bread rolls, warmed and split

1. Spray large nonstick saucepan with nonstick cooking spray; heat over medium heat. Add onion and 2 teaspoons garlic; cook and stir 5 minutes or until onion is tender. Add tomatoes with juice, bay leaves, 2 teaspoons basil, 1 teaspoon oregano, ½ teaspoon black pepper and red pepper flakes; cover and simmer 30 minutes, stirring occasionally. Remove and discard bay leaves.

2. Combine beef, green onions, bread crumbs, parsley, egg white, water, remaining 1 teaspoon garlic, ½ teaspoon basil, 1 teaspoon oregano, ¼ teaspoon black pepper, marjoram and mustard in medium bowl; mix well. Shape mixture into 16 small meatballs.

3. Spray large nonstick skillet with cooking spray; heat over medium heat. Add meatballs; cook 5 minutes or until cooked through (160°F), turning occasionally. Add meatballs to sauce; cook 5 minutes, stirring occasionally.

4. Place 4 meatballs in each roll. Spoon sauce over meatballs. Serve immediately. *Makes 4 servings*

Italian Meatball Subs

Pizza Meatball and Noodle Soup

1 can (about 14 ounces) reduced-sodium beef broth
½ cup chopped onion
½ cup chopped carrot
2 ounces uncooked whole wheat spaghetti, broken into
    2- to 3-inch pieces
1 cup zucchini slices, cut in half
½ pound frozen fully cooked Italian-style meatballs, thawed
1 can (8 ounces) tomato sauce
½ cup (2 ounces) shredded mozzarella cheese

1. Combine broth, onion, carrot and spaghetti in large saucepan; bring to a boil. Reduce heat; cover and simmer 3 minutes.

2. Add zucchini, meatballs and tomato sauce to broth mixture; return to a boil. Reduce heat; cover and simmer over medium-low heat 8 to 10 minutes or until meatballs are heated through and spaghetti is tender, stirring frequently. Sprinkle with cheese before serving.

Makes 4 servings

Meatball Hero Sandwiches

1 pound lean ground beef
½ cup Italian seasoned dry bread crumbs
1 egg
1 jar (1 pound 10 ounces) RAGÚ® Old World Style® or Chunky
    Pasta Sauce
4 Italian rolls (each about 6 inches long), halved lengthwise
½ cup shredded mozzarella cheese (about 2 ounces)

1. Combine ground beef, bread crumbs and egg in medium bowl; shape into 12 meatballs.

2. Bring Pasta Sauce to a boil in 3-quart saucepan over medium-high heat. Gently stir in uncooked meatballs.

3. Reduce heat to low and simmer covered, stirring occasionally, 20 minutes or until meatballs are done. Serve meatballs and sauce in rolls and top with cheese.

Makes 4 servings

Pizza Meatball and Noodle Soup

Spicy Meatball Sandwiches

1 large (17×15-inch) foil cooking bag
1 jar (26 ounces) marinara sauce
1 package (1 pound) frozen precooked Italian-style meatballs
½ cup chopped green bell pepper
⅓ cup sliced black olives
2 teaspoons Italian seasoning
¼ teaspoon ground red pepper
6 slices mozzarella cheese, halved lengthwise
6 hoagie buns, split
3 tablespoons finely shredded Parmesan cheese

1. Prepare grill for direct cooking.

2. Place bag on baking sheet. Combine marinara sauce, meatballs, bell pepper, olives, Italian seasoning and red pepper in large bowl. Pour into bag. Double fold open side of bag, leaving head space for heat circulation.

3. Slide bag off baking sheet onto grid. Grill, covered, over medium-hot coals 11 to 13 minutes or until meatballs are hot. Carefully open bag to allow steam to escape.

4. Place two pieces mozzarella cheese on bottom of each bun. Spoon meatball mixture onto buns; sprinkle with Parmesan cheese.

Makes 6 sandwiches

These meatballs can also be cooked in a preheated 350°F oven. Follow the recipe directions through Step 2. Place the baking sheet with the cooking bag in the oven; bake 15 minutes or until the meatballs are heated through.

Spicy Meatball Sandwich

Italian-Style Meatball Soup

½ pound ground beef
¼ pound bulk Italian sausage
 1 onion, finely chopped, divided
⅓ cup plain dry bread crumbs
 1 egg, beaten
½ teaspoon salt
 4 cups reduced-sodium vegetable or beef broth
 2 cups water
 1 can (about 8 ounces) stewed tomatoes, undrained
 1 can (8 ounces) pizza sauce
 2 cups sliced cabbage
 1 can (about 15 ounces) kidney beans, rinsed and drained
 2 carrots, sliced
½ cup frozen Italian green beans

1. Combine beef, sausage, 2 tablespoons onion, bread crumbs, egg and salt in large bowl; mix well. Shape mixture into 32 (1-inch) meatballs.

2. Brown half of meatballs in large skillet over medium heat, turning frequently. Remove from skillet; drain on paper towels. Repeat with remaining meatballs.

3. Combine broth, water, tomatoes with juice and pizza sauce in large saucepan or Dutch oven; bring to a boil over medium-high heat. Add meatballs, remaining onion, cabbage, beans and carrots; bring to a boil. Reduce heat to medium-low; simmer 20 minutes. Add green beans; simmer 10 minutes.   *Makes 8 servings*

Italian-Style Meatball Soup

Meatball Sub Sandwiches

4 sheets (12×18 inches each) REYNOLDS WRAP® Non-Stick Foil
1 package (16 ounces) frozen Italian-flavored meatballs
1 jar (27¾ ounces) chunky spaghetti sauce
4 sub or hoagie-style rolls
1 cup shredded mozzarella cheese

PREHEAT grill to medium-high or oven to 450°F.

CENTER one-fourth of meatballs on each sheet of REYNOLDS WRAP® Non-Stick Foil with non-stick (dull) side toward food. Top with spaghetti sauce.

BRING up foil sides. Double fold top and ends to seal packet, leaving room for heat circulation inside. Repeat to make four packets.

GRILL 10 to 12 minutes on covered grill **OR BAKE** 15 to 20 minutes on a cookie sheet in oven. Serve meatballs and sauce in sub rolls. Sprinkle with cheese before serving. *Makes 4 servings*

Reynolds Kitchens Tip: Heat sub rolls on the grill on a sheet of non-stick foil 2 to 3 minutes or until toasted.

Italian Meatball Hero

1½ pounds ground beef
⅓ cup grated Parmesan cheese
¼ cup dry seasoned bread crumbs
3 tablespoons FRENCH'S® Worcestershire Sauce
1 egg
2 jars (14 ounces each) spaghetti sauce
6 large Italian hero rolls, split
8 slices provolone or mozzarella cheese

1. Heat oven to 425°F. In bowl, gently mix beef, Parmesan cheese, bread crumbs, Worcestershire and egg. Shape into 1-inch meatballs. Place on rack in roasting pan. Bake for 15 minutes or until cooked.

2. In large saucepot, combine meatballs and spaghetti sauce. Cook until heated through.

3. Spoon meatballs and sauce on bottoms of rolls, dividing evenly. Top each with 2 slices provolone cheese. Close rolls.

Makes 6 servings

Meatball Sub Sandwiches

Meatball Soup

¾ pound ground turkey
1 egg white, beaten
¼ cup Italian seasoned dry bread crumbs
3 cloves garlic, minced, divided
3 teaspoons Italian seasoning, divided
¾ teaspoon whole fennel seeds, crushed
½ teaspoon salt
⅛ teaspoon black pepper
¾ cup chopped onion
8 ounces hubbard or other winter yellow squash, peeled, seeded and cut into ¾-inch pieces
3 cans (about 14 ounces each) reduced-sodium chicken broth
1 can (about 15 ounces) great Northern beans, rinsed and drained
1 can (about 15 ounces) diced tomatoes
1 cup frozen peas
4 ounces uncooked ditalini pasta
Salt and black pepper
Minced fresh parsley

1. Preheat oven to 375°F. Spray baking pan with nonstick cooking spray.

2. Combine turkey, egg white, bread crumbs, 1 clove garlic, 1 teaspoon Italian seasoning, fennel seeds, ½ teaspoon salt and ⅛ teaspoon pepper in medium bowl; mix well. Shape mixture into 18 meatballs.

3. Place meatballs in prepared pan; bake 15 to 20 minutes or until browned and cooked through (165°F). Drain on paper towels.

4. Spray large saucepan with cooking spray; heat over medium heat. Add onion, squash and remaining 2 cloves garlic; cook and stir about 5 minutes or until onion is tender. Add remaining 2 teaspoons Italian seasoning; cook 1 minute.

5. Add broth, beans, tomatoes and peas; bring to a boil. Reduce heat to medium-low; cover and simmer 5 minutes. Stir in pasta; simmer, uncovered, about 10 minutes or until pasta is tender. Add meatballs during last 5 minutes of cooking time. Season to taste with salt and pepper. Sprinkle with parsley before serving. *Makes 6 servings*

Meatball Soup

ABC Meatball Soup

Meatballs
- 1 pound ground turkey breast or extra-lean ground beef
- ¾ cup QUAKER® Oats (quick or old fashioned, uncooked)
- ⅓ cup barbecue sauce or ketchup

Soup
- 1 carton (48 ounces) reduced-sodium, fat-free chicken broth (about 6 cups)
- ¼ cup alphabet or other small shaped pasta
- 1 package (10 ounces) frozen mixed vegetables (do not thaw)

1. Heat broiler. Lightly spray rack of broiler pan with nonstick cooking spray.

2. For meatballs, combine turkey, oats and barbecue sauce in large bowl; mix lightly but thoroughly. Transfer to sheet of foil. Pat mixture into 9×6-inch rectangle. Cut into 1½-inch squares; roll each square into ball to make 24 meatballs. Arrange on broiler pan.

3. Broil 6 to 8 inches from heat about 6 minutes or until cooked through, turning once.

4. For soup, bring chicken broth to a boil in 4-quart saucepan or Dutch oven over medium-high heat. Add pasta and frozen vegetables; return to a boil. Reduce heat; cover and simmer 8 minutes or until vegetables and pasta are tender. Add meatballs and cook 1 minute. Serve immediately.

Makes 6 (1⅓-cup) servings

Tip: Garlic powder, onion powder or dried thyme may be added to the meatball ingredients.

Tip: Frozen corn, frozen green beans, frozen peas and carrots or your favorite vegetable blend may be substituted for the mixed vegetables.

ABC Meatball Soup

Meatball Grinders

1 can (about 14 ounces) diced tomatoes, drained and juice reserved
1 can (8 ounces) tomato sauce
¼ cup chopped onion
2 tablespoons tomato paste
1 teaspoon Italian seasoning
1 pound ground chicken
½ cup fresh bread crumbs (1 slice bread)
3 tablespoons finely chopped fresh parsley
1 egg white, beaten
2 cloves garlic, minced
¼ teaspoon salt
⅛ teaspoon black pepper
4 small hard rolls, split
¼ cup grated Parmesan cheese

Slow Cooker Directions

1. Combine diced tomatoes, ½ cup reserved juice, tomato sauce, onion, tomato paste and Italian seasoning in slow cooker. Cover; cook on LOW 3 to 4 hours.

2. Halfway through cooking time, prepare meatballs. Combine chicken, bread crumbs, parsley, egg white, garlic, salt and pepper in medium bowl; mix well. Shape mixture into 12 to 16 meatballs with wet hands.

3. Spray medium nonstick skillet with nonstick cooking spray; heat over medium heat. Add meatballs; cook 8 to 10 minutes or until well browned on all sides. Add meatballs to slow cooker; cook 1 to 2 hours or until meatballs are cooked through (165°F).

4. Place 3 to 4 meatballs in each roll. Spoon sauce over meatballs. Sprinkle with cheese. *Makes 4 servings*

Meatball Grinder

Pasta Meatball Soup

10 ounces ground beef
5 tablespoons uncooked acini di pepe pasta, divided (see tip)
¼ cup fresh bread crumbs
1 egg, beaten
2 tablespoons finely chopped fresh parsley, divided
1 teaspoon dried basil, divided
1 clove garlic, minced
¼ teaspoon salt
⅛ teaspoon black pepper
2 cans (about 14 ounces each) reduced-sodium beef broth
1 can (about 8 ounces) tomato sauce
⅓ cup chopped onion

1. Combine beef, 2 tablespoons pasta, bread crumbs, egg, 1 tablespoon parsley, ½ teaspoon basil, garlic, salt and pepper in medium bowl; mix well. Shape mixture into 28 to 30 (1-inch) meatballs.

2. Bring broth, tomato sauce, onion and remaining ½ teaspoon basil to a boil in large saucepan over medium-high heat. Carefully add meatballs to broth mixture. Reduce heat to medium-low; cover and simmer 20 minutes.

3. Add remaining 3 tablespoons pasta; cook 10 minutes or until tender. Sprinkle with remaining 1 tablespoon parsley.   *Makes 4 servings*

Acini di pepe is Italian for "peppercorns." This tiny rice-shaped pasta is traditionally used in soups, but pastina or orzo may be substituted.

Pasta Meatball Soup

Shanghai Meatball Soup

1 pound ground turkey
¾ cup QUAKER® Oats (quick or old fashioned, uncooked)
¼ cup reduced-sodium chicken broth
2 tablespoons reduced-sodium soy sauce
1 tablespoon dry sherry (optional)
2 teaspoons sesame oil (optional)
1½ teaspoons minced fresh ginger or ½ teaspoon ground ginger
½ teaspoon black pepper
2 cans (14½ ounces each) reduced-sodium chicken broth
1 cup water
1½ cups halved pea pods or 1 package (6 ounces) frozen pea pods, thawed, cut in half
1 cup thinly sliced carrots
1½ cups bean sprouts
¼ cup thinly sliced green onions

1. Heat broiler. Spray rack of broiler pan with nonstick cooking spray or oil lightly.

2. For meatballs, combine turkey, oats, ¼ cup broth, soy sauce, sherry and sesame oil, if desired, ginger and pepper in large bowl; mix lightly but thoroughly. Shape into 1-inch meatballs; place on rack of broiler pan.

3. Broil 6 to 8 inches from heat 7 to 10 minutes or until cooked through.

4. For soup, combine meatballs with 2 cans broth and water in 4-quart saucepan or Dutch oven; bring to a boil over high heat. Add pea pods and carrots; cook 1 to 2 minutes or until vegetables are crisp-tender. Turn off heat; add bean sprouts and green onions. Serve immediately.

Makes 6 servings

Magnificent Salsa Meatball Hoagies

1 (6.8-ounce) package RICE-A-RONI® Beef Flavor
1 pound ground beef
½ cup dry bread crumbs
1 (24-ounce) jar salsa, divided
1 large egg
6 hoagie or French rolls, split in half
   Grated Parmesan cheese (optional)

1. In large bowl, combine rice-vermicelli mix, ground beef, bread crumbs, ½ cup salsa, egg and Special Seasonings. Shape meat mixture into 24 (1½-inch) meatballs. Arrange in large skillet.

2. Add 1½ cups water and remaining salsa; bring to a boil. Reduce heat to medium. Cover; simmer 30 to 35 minutes or until rice in meatballs is tender.

3. Place 4 meatballs in each roll. Top with sauce and cheese, if desired.

Makes 6 servings

Meatball Sandwiches

1 cup PACE® Picante Sauce
1 pound ground beef
1 cup crushed tortilla chips
1 egg, beaten
1 tablespoon chopped fresh parsley or 1 teaspoon dried parsley flakes
1½ cups PREGO® Traditional or Marinara Italian Sauce
6 long hard rolls, split

1. Mix ½ cup picante sauce, beef, chips, egg and parsley thoroughly and shape firmly into 18 (1½-inch) meatballs.

2. In a 10-inch skillet over medium heat, stir the Italian sauce and remaining picante sauce. Add the meatballs and heat to a boil. Reduce heat to low. Cover and cook for 20 minutes or until the meatballs are thoroughly cooked, stirring occasionally.

3. Place the meatballs and sauce in the rolls.

Makes 6 servings

Lamb Meatball & Chickpea Soup

1 pound ground lamb
¼ cup chopped onion
1 clove garlic, minced
1 teaspoon ground cumin
½ teaspoon salt
2 cups chicken broth
1 package (10 ounces) frozen chopped broccoli*
1 tomato, peeled and chopped
1 can (about 15 ounces) chickpeas or black-eyed peas,
   rinsed and drained
½ teaspoon dried thyme
   Salt and black pepper

*You may substitute 1½ cups fresh broccoli florets for frozen chopped broccoli.

1. Combine lamb, onion, garlic, cumin and salt in medium bowl; mix well. Shape mixture into 1-inch meatballs. Brown meatballs in large skillet over medium-high heat, turning occasionally.

2. Meanwhile, bring broth to a boil in large saucepan over high heat. Add broccoli and tomato; bring to a boil.

3. Reduce heat to medium-low. Add meatballs, chickpeas and thyme; cover and simmer 5 minutes. Season with salt and pepper.

Makes 4 to 6 servings

Tip: To quickly shape uniform meatballs, place the lamb mixture on a cutting board and pat evenly into a square about 1 inch thick. Cut into 1-inch squares; shape each square into a ball.

Lamb Meatball & Chickpea Soup

Open-Face Meatball Subs

½ pound ground beef
¼ pound bulk turkey Italian sausage
½ package (10 ounces) frozen chopped spinach, thawed
    and squeezed dry
8 shredded wheat crackers, finely crushed
1 egg, beaten
3 teaspoons dried basil, divided
1⅓ cups prepared pasta sauce
1 whole wheat baguette, cut in half lengthwise, then cut
    in half crosswise
1 clove garlic, cut in half crosswise

1. Combine beef, sausage, spinach, cracker crumbs, egg and 1 teaspoon basil in medium bowl; mix well. Shape mixture into 16 meatballs.

2. Spray medium nonstick skillet with nonstick cooking spray; heat over medium-high heat. Add meatballs; cook 5 minutes or until beginning to brown, turning frequently.

3. Add pasta sauce and remaining 2 teaspoons basil to skillet; bring to a boil over medium-high heat. Stir gently. Reduce heat to medium-low; cover and simmer about 8 minutes or until meatballs are cooked through (160°F).

4. Preheat broiler. Place bread under broiler until lightly toasted. Rub cut sides of bread with cut sides of garlic. Place 4 meatballs on each bread slice; top with sauce. *Makes 4 servings*

Open-Face Meatball Sub

Quick & Easy Meatball Soup

1 package (about 1 pound) frozen Italian sausage meatballs without sauce
2 cans (about 14 ounces each) Italian-style stewed tomatoes, undrained
2 cans (about 14 ounces each) reduced-sodium beef broth
1 can (about 14 ounces) mixed vegetables
½ cup uncooked rotini pasta or small macaroni
½ teaspoon dried oregano

1. Thaw meatballs in microwave according to package directions.

2. Combine tomatoes with juice, broth, vegetables, pasta and oregano in large saucepan. Add meatballs; bring to a boil. Reduce heat; cover and simmer over medium-low heat 15 minutes or until pasta is tender.

Makes 4 to 6 servings

Mozzarella Meatball Sandwiches

1 loaf (11.75 ounces) PEPPERIDGE FARM® Frozen Mozzarella Garlic Cheese Bread
½ cup PREGO® Traditional Italian Sauce or PREGO® Organic Tomato & Basil Italian Sauce
12 (½-ounce) or 6 (1-ounce) frozen meatballs

1. Heat the oven to 400°F. Remove the bread from the bag. Carefully separate the bread halves with a fork. Place the **2** bread halves, cut-side up, onto a baking sheet.

2. Bake for 10 minutes or until the bread is heated through.

3. Heat the Italian sauce and meatballs in a 2-quart saucepan over low heat. Cook and stir for 20 minutes or until the meatballs are heated through. Spoon the meatball mixture onto the bottom bread half. Top with the top bread half. Cut into quarters. *Makes 4 servings*

Prep Time: 15 minutes • **Bake Time:** 10 minutes • **Cook Time:** 20 minutes

Quick & Easy Meatball Soup

International Intrigue

Greek-Style Meatballs and Spinach

½ cup old-fashioned oats
¼ cup minced onion
1 clove garlic, minced
¼ teaspoon dried oregano
⅛ teaspoon black pepper
1 egg, beaten
½ pound ground lamb
1 cup reduced-sodium beef broth
¼ teaspoon salt
½ cup plain yogurt
1 teaspoon all-purpose flour
4 cups baby spinach, coarsely chopped
2 cups cooked egg noodles

Slow Cooker Directions

1. Combine oats, onion, garlic, oregano and pepper in medium bowl. Stir in egg. Add lamb; mix well. Shape mixture into 16 meatballs. Place in slow cooker.

2. Add broth and salt to slow cooker. Cover; cook on LOW 6 hours.

3. Whisk yogurt and flour in small bowl until well blended. Stir about ¼ cup hot liquid from slow cooker into yogurt. Stir yogurt mixture back into slow cooker. Stir in spinach. Cover; cook 10 minutes or until heated through. Serve over noodles. *Makes 4 servings*

Middle Eastern Turkey Meatballs with Couscous

1 cup finely chopped onion, divided
1 cup reduced-sodium chicken broth
⅔ cup uncooked whole wheat or plain couscous
½ teaspoon salt, divided
1 cup baby spinach
¾ pound ground turkey
1 egg, beaten
1 tablespoon steak sauce
¾ teaspoon ground cinnamon
¾ teaspoon ground cumin
¼ teaspoon black pepper
½ cup water
2 tablespoons tomato paste

1. Spray large skillet with nonstick cooking spray; heat over medium heat. Add ¾ cup onion; cook and stir 4 minutes or until tender. Remove from skillet.

2. Bring broth to a boil in small saucepan over high heat; stir in couscous and ¼ teaspoon salt. Remove from heat; cover and let stand 5 minutes. Stir in cooked onion and spinach.

3. Meanwhile, combine turkey, egg, remaining ¼ cup onion, steak sauce, cinnamon, cumin, remaining ¼ teaspoon salt and pepper in medium bowl; mix well. Shape mixture into 24 (1-inch) meatballs.

4. Spray same skillet with cooking spray; heat over medium-high heat. Add meatballs; cook about 7 minutes or until cooked through (165°F), turning frequently to brown on all sides. Transfer meatballs to plate; keep warm.

5. Add water and tomato paste to skillet; whisk until blended. Bring to a boil; reduce heat to low. Add meatballs; cook until heated through. Serve meatballs over couscous. *Makes 4 servings*

Middle Eastern Turkey Meatballs with Couscous

Thai Coconut Chicken Meatballs

1 pound ground chicken
2 green onions, chopped
2 teaspoons mirin
2 teaspoons toasted sesame oil
1 teaspoon fish sauce
1 clove garlic, minced
1 tablespoon canola oil
½ cup unsweetened canned coconut milk
¼ cup chicken broth
1 teaspoon Thai red curry paste
2 teaspoons packed brown sugar
2 teaspoons lime juice
2 tablespoons cold water
1 tablespoon cornstarch

Slow Cooker Directions

1. Combine chicken, green onions, mirin, sesame oil, fish sauce and garlic in large bowl; mix well. Shape mixture into 1½-inch meatballs.

2. Heat canola oil in large skillet over medium-high heat. Add meatballs; cook until brown on all sides. Transfer to slow cooker. Add coconut milk, broth, curry paste and brown sugar. Cover; cook on HIGH 3½ to 4 hours. Stir in lime juice.

3. Stir cold water and cornstarch in small bowl until smooth. Stir into sauce in slow cooker. Cook, uncovered, 10 to 15 minutes or until sauce is slightly thickened and evenly coats meatballs.   *Makes 4 to 5 servings*

Tip: Meatballs that are of equal size will cook at the same rate and be done at the same time. To ensure that your meatballs are the same size, pat the meat mixture into an even rectangle, then cut into even rows and columns. Roll each portion into a smooth ball.

Thai Coconut Chicken Meatballs

Barbecued Swedish Meatballs

Meatballs
- 1½ pounds lean ground beef
- 1 cup finely chopped onion
- ½ cup fresh bread crumbs
- ½ cup HOLLAND HOUSE® White Cooking Wine
- 1 egg, beaten
- ½ teaspoon ground allspice
- ½ teaspoon ground nutmeg

Sauce
- 1 jar (10 ounces) currant jelly
- ½ cup chili sauce
- ¼ cup HOLLAND HOUSE® White Cooking Wine
- 1 tablespoon cornstarch

Heat oven to 350°F. In medium bowl, combine all meatball ingredients; mix well. Shape into 1-inch balls. Place meatballs in 15×10×1-inch baking pan. Bake 20 minutes or until brown.

In medium saucepan, combine all sauce ingredients; mix well. Cook over medium heat until mixture boils and thickens, stirring occasionally. Add meatballs. To serve, place meatballs and sauce in fondue pot or chafing dish. *Makes 6 to 8 servings*

Salsa Verde Meatballs

- 1¼ cups PACE® Salsa Verde
- 1½ pounds ground beef
- 1 egg
- ¾ cup finely crushed tortilla chips
- 4 green onions, minced (about ½ cup)

1. Heat the oven to 350°F.

2. Thoroughly mix ¾ cup salsa, beef, egg, tortilla chips and green onions in a large bowl. Shape the mixture firmly into **16** meatballs.

3. Place the meatballs into a 3-quart shallow baking dish. Top each with 1 teaspoon salsa.

4. Bake for 20 minutes or until the meatballs are cooked through. Serve with the remaining salsa. *Makes 16 servings*

Barbecued Swedish Meatballs

Koftas (Lamb Meatballs in Spicy Gravy)

1½ pounds ground lamb or ground beef
1½ cups finely chopped onions, divided
2 eggs, beaten
½ cup chopped fresh cilantro
2 cloves garlic, minced
2 teaspoons garam masala
1½ teaspoons salt, divided
1 teaspoon minced fresh ginger
24 whole blanched almonds
1 tablespoon peanut oil
1 teaspoon *each* ground coriander, ground cumin and chili powder
½ teaspoon turmeric
2 tomatoes, peeled, seeded and chopped
½ cup water
1 cup plain yogurt

1. Place lamb, ½ cup onion, eggs, cilantro, garlic, garam masala, ½ teaspoon salt and ginger in medium bowl; mix well. Refrigerate at least 1 hour or overnight.

2. Shape mixture into 24 ovals or balls; insert 1 almond into each meatball. Heat oil in large skillet over medium-high heat. Add half of meatballs; cook 8 minutes or until brown on all sides. Remove from skillet; repeat with remaining meatballs.

3. Add remaining 1 cup onion to skillet; cook and stir over medium heat 6 to 8 minutes or until browned. Stir in remaining 1 teaspoon salt, coriander, cumin, chili powder and turmeric. Add tomatoes; cook and stir 5 minutes or until tomatoes are tender.

4. Add water; bring to a boil over high heat. Add meatballs. Reduce heat to medium-low; simmer 15 minutes or until cooked through (160°F). Remove meatballs to serving platter; keep warm.

5. Remove skillet from heat. Place yogurt in small bowl; stir several spoonfuls hot sauce mixture from skillet into yogurt. Stir yogurt mixture back into skillet; cook over medium-low heat until sauce thickens. *Do not boil.* Pour sauce over meatballs. *Makes 6 servings*

Spicy Caribbean Meatballs

1 pound extra lean ground beef
½ cup fine dry bread crumbs
1 egg or ¼ cup egg substitute
1 can (10½ ounces) condensed beef consommé, divided
1 teaspoon pumpkin pie spice
Salt and black pepper to taste
¼ cup finely chopped onion
¼ cup finely chopped green bell pepper
½ jalapeño pepper, finely chopped
Water

1. In large bowl combine bread crumbs, egg and ¼ cup consommé. Add pumpkin pie spice and salt and black pepper to taste. Blend well.

2. Add ground beef, onion, bell pepper and jalapeño pepper to crumb mixture and mix lightly. Form into 1½- to 2-inch meatballs.

3. Place meatballs on baking sheet coated with nonstick cooking spray. Brown under preheated broiler, turning once.

4. Transfer meatballs to large skillet; add ¼ cup consommé and ¼ cup water. Bring to a simmer; cook about 15 minutes or until cooked through, adding water if necessary. *Makes 4 servings*

Tips: Remaining consommé can be used to make gravy, if desired. Meatballs can be made smaller and served as an appetizer.

Favorite recipe from **North Dakota Beef Commission**

Greek Coffee Meatballs

1 tablespoon olive oil
1 small onion, minced
4 slices rustic bread, crusts removed, cut into ½-inch pieces
1 cup brewed coffee
1 pound ground beef
¼ cup chopped fresh mint
¼ cup chopped fresh Italian parsley
1½ tablespoons crumbled feta cheese
2 teaspoons red wine vinegar
1 teaspoon minced fresh oregano
¾ teaspoon salt
¼ teaspoon black pepper
½ cup finely chopped blanched almonds
½ cup all-purpose flour
Vegetable oil
Additional chopped fresh Italian parsley (optional)

1. Heat olive oil in small skillet over medium-high heat. Add onion; cook and stir over medium heat until golden. *Do not brown.*

2. Place bread slices in bowl; Pour in coffee. Let soak about 5 minutes or until bread is soft. Remove bread; squeeze out excess liquid.

3. Combine onion, bread, beef, mint, parsley, cheese, vinegar, oregano, salt and pepper in large bowl; mix well. Cover with plastic wrap and refrigerate at least 2 hours or overnight.

4. Shape mixture into 24 golf ball-sized meatballs. Place almonds and flour in separate shallow dishes. Roll meatballs in almonds, then in flour.

5. Pour vegetable oil into large skillet to depth of ½ inch; heat over medium-high heat. Cook meatballs in single layer until browned on all sides and cooked through (160°F), cooking in batches if necessary. Drain meatballs on paper towels. Garnish with additional parsley.

Makes 2 dozen meatballs

Greek Coffee Meatballs

Pork Meatballs in Garlicky Almond Sauce

½ cup blanched whole almonds
1 cup chicken broth
⅓ cup roasted red pepper
4 teaspoons minced garlic, divided
1 teaspoon salt, divided
½ teaspoon saffron threads (optional)
1 cup fresh bread crumbs, divided
¼ cup dry white wine or chicken broth
1 pound ground pork
¼ cup finely chopped onion
1 egg, beaten
3 tablespoons minced fresh parsley

1. Preheat oven to 350°F. Line shallow baking pans with foil; lightly spray with nonstick cooking spray.

2. Place almonds in food processor; process until finely ground. Add broth, red pepper, 2 teaspoons garlic, ½ teaspoon salt and saffron, if desired; process until smooth. Stir in ¼ cup bread crumbs.

3. Place remaining ¾ cup bread crumbs in large bowl; sprinkle with wine and stir gently. Add pork, onion, egg, parsley, remaining 2 teaspoons garlic and ½ teaspoon salt; mix well. Shape mixture into 24 (1-inch) meatballs. Place meatballs in prepared pans, spacing about 1 inch apart. Bake about 20 minutes or until lightly browned.

4. Transfer meatballs to 1½-quart shallow casserole. Pour sauce over meatballs. Bake 25 to 30 minutes or until sauce is bubbly.

Makes 6 servings

Pork Meatballs in Garlicky Almond Sauce

Mu Shu Meatball Wraps

Meatballs
  1 pound lean ground turkey or lean ground beef
  ¾ cup QUAKER® Oats (quick or old fashioned, uncooked)
  ½ cup finely chopped water chestnuts
  ⅓ cup chopped green onions
  1 clove garlic, minced
  1 teaspoon finely chopped fresh ginger or ¼ teaspoon ground
      ginger
  ¼ cup light soy sauce
  1 tablespoon water
Wraps
  ¾ cup prepared plum sauce
  6 (10-inch) flour tortillas, warmed
  1½ cups coleslaw mix or combination of shredded cabbage
      and shredded carrots

1. Heat oven to 350°F. Combine all meatball ingredients in large bowl; mix lightly but thoroughly. Shape into 24 (1½-inch) meatballs; arrange on rack of broiler pan.

2. Bake 20 to 25 minutes or until no longer pink in centers (170°F for turkey; 160°F for beef).

3. To prepare wraps, spread plum sauce on flour tortilla; add about ¼ cup coleslaw mix and 4 hot meatballs. Fold sides of tortilla to center, overlapping edges; fold bottom and top of tortilla under, completely enclosing filling. Repeat with remaining ingredients. Cut wraps in half to serve. *Makes 6 servings*

Mu Shu Meatball Wraps

Pork Meatballs & Sauerkraut

1¼ pounds ground pork
¾ cup plain dry bread crumbs
1 egg, beaten
2 tablespoons milk
2 teaspoons caraway seeds, divided
1 teaspoon salt
½ teaspoon Worcestershire sauce
¼ teaspoon black pepper
1 jar (32 ounces) sauerkraut, drained, squeezed dry and chopped
6 slices bacon, crisp-cooked and crumbled
½ cup chopped onion
Chopped fresh parsley (optional)

Slow Cooker Directions

1. Combine pork, bread crumbs, egg, milk, 1 teaspoon caraway seeds, salt, Worcestershire sauce and pepper in large bowl; mix well. Shape mixture into 2-inch meatballs.

2. Brown meatballs in large nonstick skillet over medium-high heat.

3. Combine sauerkraut, bacon, onion and remaining 1 teaspoon caraway seeds in slow cooker. Place meatballs on top of sauerkraut mixture.

4. Cover; cook on LOW 6 to 8 hours. Sprinkle with parsley before serving.

Makes 4 to 6 servings

A quick and easy way to cut sauerkraut into
small pieces is to use kitchen scissors.

103

Pork Meatballs & Sauerkraut

Thai Meatballs and Noodles

Thai Meatballs (recipe follows)
12 ounces uncooked rice noodles or egg noodles
2 cans (about 14 ounces each) reduced-sodium chicken broth
2 tablespoons packed brown sugar
2 tablespoons fish sauce or reduced-sodium soy sauce
1 small piece (about 1 × ½ inch) fresh ginger, cut into thin strips
1 medium carrot, cut into matchstick-size pieces
1 pound bok choy, cut into ½-inch-wide strips
½ cup chopped fresh mint, basil or cilantro

1. Prepare Thai Meatballs. While meatballs are cooking, cook noodles according to package directions; drain and keep warm.

2. Heat broth in large saucepan over high heat. Add brown sugar, fish sauce and ginger; stir until sugar is dissolved. Add meatballs and carrot to saucepan; bring to a boil. Reduce heat to medium-low; cover and simmer 15 minutes or until meatballs are heated through.

3. Add bok choy; simmer 4 to 5 minutes or until stalks are crisp-tender. Stir in mint; serve mixture over noodles.   *Makes 6 servings*

Thai Meatballs

1½ pounds ground beef or pork
¼ cup chopped fresh basil leaves
¼ cup chopped fresh mint leaves
2 tablespoons finely chopped fresh ginger
6 cloves garlic, minced
1 tablespoon fish sauce
1 teaspoon ground cinnamon
½ teaspoon whole fennel seeds, crushed
½ teaspoon black pepper
2 tablespoons peanut oil, divided

1. Combine all ingredients except oil in large bowl; mix well. Rub cutting board with 1 tablespoon oil; pat meat mixture into 12×8-inch rectangle on board. Cut into 32 squares; shape each square into a ball.

2. Heat remaining 1 tablespoon oil in large skillet over medium-high heat. Add meatballs in single layer; cook 8 to 10 minutes or until cooked through (160°F), turning to brown all sides. (Cook in batches.) Drain on paper towels.   *Makes 32 meatballs*

Thai Meatballs and Noodles

Mediterranean Meatball Ratatouille

1 pound bulk mild Italian sausage
1 package (8 ounces) sliced mushrooms
1 small eggplant, diced
1 zucchini, diced
½ cup chopped onion
1 clove garlic, minced
1 teaspoon dried oregano
1 teaspoon salt
½ teaspoon black pepper
2 tomatoes, diced
1 tablespoon tomato paste
2 tablespoons chopped fresh basil
1 teaspoon fresh lemon juice

Slow Cooker Directions

1. Shape sausage into 1-inch meatballs. Brown meatballs in large skillet over medium heat. Place half of meatballs in slow cooker.

2. Add half each of mushrooms, eggplant and zucchini to slow cooker. Top with onion, garlic, ½ teaspoon oregano, ½ teaspoon salt and ¼ teaspoon pepper. Repeat layers with remaining meatballs, mushrooms, eggplant, zucchini, ½ teaspoon oregano, ½ teaspoon salt and ¼ teaspoon pepper. Cover; cook on LOW 6 to 7 hours.

3. Stir in tomatoes and tomato paste. Cover; cook 15 minutes. Stir in basil and lemon juice just before serving. *Makes 6 servings*

Mediterranean Meatball Ratatouille

Lamb Meatballs with Tomato Mint Dip

1 ½ cups fine bulgur wheat
3 cups cold water
2 pounds ground American lamb
1 cup minced fresh parsley
2 medium onions, minced
1 tablespoon salt
½ teaspoon ground allspice
½ teaspoon ground cinnamon
½ teaspoon ground nutmeg
½ teaspoon black pepper
¼ to ½ teaspoon ground red pepper (to taste)
1 piece fresh ginger, about 2×1 inch, peeled and minced
1 cup ice water
Tomato Mint Dip (recipe follows)

Place bulgur in medium bowl: add cold water. Let soak about 10 minutes. Drain and place in fine-meshed strainer; squeeze out water.

In large bowl, knead lamb with parsley, onions, seasonings and ginger. Add bulgur; knead well. Add enough ice water to keep mixture smooth. Use about 1 teaspoon meat mixture to make bite-sized meatballs. Place on ungreased jelly-roll pan. Bake in preheated 375°F oven 20 minutes. Meanwhile, prepare Tomato Mint Dip.

Place meatballs in serving bowl; keep warm. Serve hot with dip.

Makes 10 dozen meatballs

Tomato Mint Dip

2 cans (15 ounces each) tomato sauce with tomato bits
1 ½ teaspoons ground allspice
1 teaspoon dried mint

In small saucepan, heat all ingredients about 5 minutes to blend flavors.

Favorite recipe from **American Lamb Board**

Polynesian Meatballs

1 can (20 ounces) DOLE® Crushed Pineapple, divided
1 package (20 ounces) ground turkey or chicken
2 cups instant brown rice, uncooked
¾ cup thinly sliced green onions, divided
½ cup teriyaki sauce, divided
1 egg lightly beaten
1 teaspoon ground ginger
½ teaspoon ground nutmeg
2 tablespoons orange marmalade

• Preheat oven to 350°F.

• Drain well ½ cup crushed pineapple for meatballs. Reserve remaining pineapple and juice for sauce.

• Combine ground turkey, 2 cups rice, ½ cup drained pineapple, ½ cup green onions, ¼ cup teriyaki sauce, egg, ginger and nutmeg in large bowl, mixing well.

• Scoop about ¼ cup turkey mixture and gently roll into desired meatball size; place on aluminum foil-lined baking sheet with sides. Repeat with remaining mixture. Bake at 350°F 25 to 30 minutes.

• Meanwhile, to make sauce, combine remaining pineapple and juice, ¼ cup teriyaki sauce and orange marmalade in medium saucepan; heat to boiling. Reduce heat and simmer, uncovered, 3 to 4 minutes. Stir in remaining ¼ cup green onions.

• Top meatballs with sauce. Serve over additional cooked rice and green onions, if desired.   *Makes 15 to 16 meatballs (5 to 6 servings)*

Prep Time: 20 minutes • **Bake Time:** 30 minutes

Swedish Meatballs

1½ cups fresh bread crumbs
1 cup whipping cream
2 tablespoons butter, divided
1 small onion, chopped
1 pound ground beef
½ pound ground pork
3 tablespoons chopped fresh parsley, divided
1½ teaspoons salt
¼ teaspoon ground allspice
¼ teaspoon black pepper
1 cup beef broth
1 cup sour cream
1 tablespoon all-purpose flour

1. Combine bread crumbs and cream in small bowl; mix well. Let stand 10 minutes.

2. Melt 1 tablespoon butter in large skillet over medium heat. Add onion; cook and stir 5 minutes or until onion is tender.

3. Combine beef, pork, bread crumb mixture, onion, 2 tablespoons parsley, salt, allspice and pepper in large bowl; mix well. Cover and refrigerate 1 hour.

4. Pat meat mixture into 1-inch-thick square on cutting board. Cut into 36 squares. Shape each square into a ball. Melt remaining 1 tablespoon butter in same skillet over medium heat. Add meatballs; cook 10 minutes or until brown on all sides and cooked through (160°F). Drain meatballs on paper towels.

5. Drain drippings from skillet; discard. Pour broth into skillet. Heat over medium-high heat, stirring frequently to scrape up browned bits.

6. Combine sour cream and flour in small bowl; mix well. Stir sour cream mixture into skillet; cook over low heat 5 minutes, stirring constantly. *Do not boil.* Add meatballs; cook 5 minutes. Sprinkle with remaining 1 tablespoon parsley.   *Makes 4 to 6 servings*

Note: Serve these meatballs with egg noodles, mashed potatoes or boiled red potatoes.

International Intrigue

Swedish Meatballs

Meatballs with a Twist

Beer-Braised Meatballs

1 pound ground beef
½ cup Italian seasoned dry bread crumbs
½ cup grated Parmesan cheese
2 eggs, beaten
⅓ cup finely chopped onion
2 cloves garlic, minced
½ teaspoon black pepper
¼ teaspoon salt
1 bottle (12 ounces) lager
1½ cups tomato sauce
1 cup ketchup
½ cup packed brown sugar
2 tablespoons tomato paste

1. Preheat oven to 400°F. Line broiler pan with foil; spray rack with nonstick cooking spray.

2. Combine beef, bread crumbs, cheese, eggs, onion, garlic, pepper and salt in large bowl; mix well. Shape mixture into 1-inch meatballs.

3. Place meatballs on broiler rack. Bake 10 minutes or until browned.

4. Bring lager, tomato sauce, ketchup, brown sugar and tomato paste to a boil in large saucepan or Dutch oven. Add meatballs; cover and simmer over low heat, stirring occasionally, 20 to 30 minutes or until meatballs are cooked through (160°F). *Makes 20 meatballs*

Turkey Meatballs with Spaghetti Squash

⅓ cup fresh whole wheat bread crumbs (1 slice bread)
¼ cup grated onion
2½ tablespoons minced Italian parsley
1 teaspoon garlic powder
1 teaspoon dried thyme
½ teaspoon whole fennel seeds
½ teaspoon red pepper flakes
1 pound ground turkey
2 egg whites, beaten
1 spaghetti squash (12 to 16 ounces)
1 can (about 14 ounces) crushed tomatoes
¼ cup reduced-sodium chicken broth
⅓ cup minced green onions
1 tablespoon minced fresh basil
1 teaspoon dried oregano

1. Mix bread crumbs, onion, parsley, garlic powder, thyme, fennel seeds and red pepper flakes in small bowl. Combine turkey, egg whites and bread crumb mixture in large bowl; mix well. Cover and refrigerate 10 minutes.

2. Meanwhile, split squash in half; remove seeds. Place in glass baking dish, cut side down. Add 3 to 4 tablespoons water; microwave on HIGH 10 to 12 minutes or until fork-tender.

3. Preheat broiler. Shape turkey mixture into 20 meatballs. Place meatballs on broiler pan; broil 4 to 5 minutes. Turn meatballs; broil 4 minutes.

4. Combine tomatoes and broth in large skillet; bring to a simmer over low heat. Add meatballs, green onions, basil and oregano; cook and stir about 10 minutes or until heated through.

5. Scrape squash into strands onto serving plates; top with meatballs and sauce. *Makes 4 servings*

Turkey Meatballs with Spaghetti Squash

Meatballs in Burgundy Sauce

60 frozen fully cooked meatballs, partially thawed and separated
3 cups chopped onions
1½ cups water
1 cup Burgundy or other red wine
¼ cup ketchup
2 packages (about 1 ounce each) beef gravy mix
1 tablespoon dried oregano
1 package (8 ounces) uncooked egg noodles

Slow Cooker Directions

1. Combine meatballs, onions, water, wine, ketchup, gravy mix and oregano in slow cooker; stir to blend.

2. Cover; cook on HIGH 4 to 5 hours.

3. Cook noodles according to package directions; drain. Serve meatballs over noodles. *Makes 6 to 8 servings*

Sweet 'n Tangy Meatballs

1 tablespoon olive oil
1 small red onion, cut into chunks
1 small red bell pepper, cut into chunks
1 jar (1 pound 10 ounces) RAGÚ® Old World Style® Pasta Sauce
1 can (8 ounces) pineapple chunks in natural juice, drained
    (reserve 1 tablespoon juice)
1 jar (12 ounces) grape jelly
1 package (20 ounces) frozen fully-cooked cocktail-size meatballs, thawed

1. In 12-inch skillet, heat olive oil over medium-high heat and cook onion and red pepper, stirring occasionally, 4 minutes or until crisp-tender. Remove vegetables and set aside.

2. In same skillet, stir in Pasta Sauce, 1 tablespoon reserved pineapple juice and jelly. Bring to a boil over medium-high heat. Gently stir in meatballs. Reduce heat and simmer, stirring occasionally, 10 minutes or until meatballs are done and sauce is thickened. Return vegetables to skillet. Stir in pineapple chunks and heat through. Serve over hot cooked rice, if desired. *Makes 6 servings*

Meatballs with a Twist

Meatballs in Burgundy Sauce

Veggie "Meatballs"

½ cup water
¾ cup bulgur wheat
2 teaspoons olive oil
3 medium portobello mushrooms (10 ounces), stemmed and diced
1 small onion, chopped
1 small zucchini, coarsely grated
1 teaspoon dried Italian seasoning
2 cloves garlic, minced
¼ cup sun-dried tomatoes (not packed in oil),* chopped
4 ounces grated Parmesan cheese
1 egg, beaten
2 cups marinara sauce, heated

*If unavailable, you can substitute ¼ cup sun-dried tomatoes packed in oil, well drained, patted dry and chopped.

1. Preheat oven to 375°F. Line baking sheet with foil; spray with nonstick cooking spray.

2. Bring water to a boil in small saucepan; remove from heat. Stir in bulgur; cover and let stand while preparing vegetables.

3. Heat oil in large nonstick skillet over medium-high heat. Add mushrooms, onion, zucchini and Italian seasoning; cook and stir about 8 minutes or until softened. Add garlic; cook and stir 1 minute. Stir in tomatoes.

4. Transfer mushroom mixture to large bowl; let cool slightly. Add bulgur, cheese and egg; mix well. Shape mixture into 12 meatballs, using ¼ cup for each. Place meatballs in prepared pan.

5. Bake 20 minutes. Turn meatballs; bake 8 to 10 minutes or until well browned. Serve with marinara sauce. *Makes 4 servings*

Veggie "Meatballs"

Orange & Port Glazed
Turkey Meatballs

4 tablespoons I CAN'T BELIEVE IT'S NOT BUTTER!® Spread, divided
½ cup finely chopped onion
1 rib celery, finely chopped (about ¼ cup)
1 pound ground turkey
1 egg
¼ cup plain dry bread crumbs
¼ cup dried cranberries, chopped
½ teaspoon finely chopped fresh thyme leaves OR ⅛ teaspoon dried
     thyme leaves, crushed
½ teaspoon salt
⅛ teaspoon ground black pepper
½ cup orange marmalade
2 tablespoons port wine or grape juice
1 teaspoon apple cider vinegar
¼ teaspoon ground cinnamon (optional)

Melt 2 tablespoons I CAN'T BELIEVE IT'S NOT BUTTER!® Spread in 12-inch nonstick skillet over medium-high heat and cook onion and celery, stirring frequently, 5 minutes or until vegetables are tender. Remove from heat and cool slightly. Combine ground turkey, egg, bread crumbs, cranberries, onion mixture, thyme, salt and pepper in medium bowl; shape into 44 (1-inch) meatballs.

Melt 1 tablespoon Spread in same skillet and brown ½ of the meatballs over medium heat, turning frequently, 7 minutes or until golden brown and almost cooked. Remove meatballs and set aside; repeat with remaining Spread and meatballs. Return meatballs to skillet, then stir in marmalade blended with port, vinegar and cinnamon. Cook over medium heat, stirring gently, 5 minutes or until sauce is thickened and meatballs are cooked.

Makes about 44 meatballs

Tip: The meatball mixture can be made up to 1 day ahead and refrigerated. The meatballs will be easier to shape if the mixture is very cold.

Prep Time: 30 minutes • **Cook Time:** 25 minutes

Meatball Veggie Kabobs

1 each green and red bell pepper, stems and seeds removed,
    cut into 1¼-inch pieces
1 yellow squash, cut lengthwise in half and then into 1¼-inch pieces
¼ cup reduced-fat vinaigrette-style Caesar salad dressing, divided
1 pound 90% lean ground beef
¾ cup QUAKER® Oats (quick or old fashioned, uncooked)
1 egg, lightly beaten
¼ cup fat-free (skim) milk
3 tablespoons finely chopped onion
1 tablespoon finely chopped garlic
1 teaspoon dried thyme leaves
1 teaspoon salt
½ teaspoon black pepper
    Shredded Parmesan cheese (optional)

1. Heat broiler. Lightly spray rack of broiler pan with nonstick cooking spray. If using bamboo skewers, soak skewers in water. Toss bell peppers and squash with 2 tablespoons dressing in medium bowl. Set aside.

2. Combine beef, oats, egg, milk, onion, garlic, thyme, salt and pepper in large bowl; mix lightly but thoroughly. Shape mixture into 20 meatballs, about 1½ inches in diameter. Alternately thread meatballs and vegetables onto eight 12-inch bamboo or metal skewers. Arrange kabobs on broiler pan. Drizzle with any dressing remaining in medium bowl.

3. Broil 3 to 4 inches from heat, until meatballs are cooked through (160°F) and vegetables are tender, about 10 minutes, turning once and brushing with remaining 2 tablespoons dressing.

4. Serve kabobs sprinkled with cheese, if desired.   *Makes 4 servings*

Good Stuff Meatballs

1 pound ground beef
⅓ cup quick oats
⅓ cup finely chopped baby spinach
1 egg, beaten
¼ cup grated Parmesan cheese
½ teaspoon salt
⅛ teaspoon black pepper
1 teaspoon olive oil
¼ cup shredded carrot
1½ cups pasta sauce
    Additional grated Parmesan cheese (optional)

1. Preheat oven to 400°F.

2. Combine beef, oats, spinach, egg, ¼ cup cheese, salt and pepper in medium bowl; mix well. Shape mixture into 24 meatballs. Place in 13×9-inch baking dish. Bake 23 to 25 minutes or until cooked through (160°F).

3. Heat oil in medium saucepan. Add carrot; cook and stir over medium heat 2 minutes. Add pasta sauce; bring to a boil. Reduce heat to low; simmer 5 minutes.

4. Serve meatballs with sauce and toothpicks for dipping, or serve meatballs and sauce over pasta or rice and sprinkle with additional cheese.   *Makes 4 servings*

Quick-cooking oats and old-fashioned oats provide the same nutrients and fiber; the quick oats simply cook faster because they have been rolled into thinner flakes.

Meatballs with a Twist

Good Stuff Meatballs

Nancy's Grilled Turkey Meatballs

1 pound lean ground turkey breast
½ cup oatmeal
¼ cup fresh whole wheat bread crumbs
1 egg white
3 tablespoons fat-free or reduced-fat Parmesan cheese
2 tablespoons FRENCH'S® Honey Dijon Mustard
¼ teaspoon crushed garlic
¼ teaspoon ground black pepper
1 cup pineapple chunks or wedges
1 small red bell pepper, cut into squares

1. Combine turkey, oatmeal, bread crumbs, egg white, cheese, mustard, garlic and black pepper in large bowl. Mix well and form into 24 meatballs.

2. Place 4 meatballs on each skewer, alternating with pineapple and bell pepper.

3. Cook meatballs 10 minutes on well-greased grill over medium heat until no longer pink inside, turning often. Serve with additional FRENCH'S® Honey Dijon Mustard on the side for dipping.   *Makes 6 servings*

Tip: Combine ⅓ cup *each* FRENCH'S® Honey Dijon Mustard, honey and FRANK'S® REDHOT® Cayenne Pepper Sauce. Use for dipping meatballs, grilled wings, ribs and chicken.

Prep Time: 15 minutes • **Cook Time:** 10 minutes

Meatballs with a Twist

Nancy's Grilled Turkey Meatballs

Earth's Core Meatballs

3 to 4 ounces mozzarella cheese, cut into ¼- to ½-inch cubes
25 medium to large cherry tomatoes, halved and seeded
2 eggs, divided
2 pounds ground beef
1½ cups Italian seasoned dry bread crumbs, divided
1 teaspoon salt
¾ teaspoon garlic powder
½ teaspoon black pepper
Hot cooked pasta
Pasta sauce, heated

1. Preheat oven to 350°F. Line two baking sheets with foil; spray generously with nonstick cooking spray.

2. Place one cheese cube inside one tomato half; cover with another tomato half to encase cheese.

3. Lightly beat one egg in large bowl. Add beef, ½ cup bread crumbs, salt, garlic powder and pepper; mix well. Shape 2 tablespoons beef mixture into 2-inch circle. Place cheese-filled tomato in center, then bring edges of circle together to completely encase tomato. Lightly roll meatball with hands to form smooth ball. Place on prepared baking sheet. Repeat with remaining beef mixture and tomatoes.

4. Lightly beat remaining egg in medium shallow bowl. Place remaining 1 cup bread crumbs in another shallow bowl. Dip meatballs, one at a time, into beaten egg; shake off excess and roll in bread crumbs to coat. Return to baking sheets.

5. Bake 35 minutes or until meatballs are slightly crisp and cooked through (160°F), turning halfway through baking time. Serve with pasta and sauce.

Makes 12 servings

Meatballs with a Twist

Earth's Core Meatballs

Chicken Meatballs with Chipotle-Honey Sauce

2 pounds ground chicken
2 eggs, beaten
1/3 cup plain dry bread crumbs
1/3 cup chopped fresh cilantro
2 tablespoons fresh lime juice
4 cloves garlic, minced
1 can (4 ounces) chipotle peppers in adobo sauce, divided
1 teaspoon salt
   Chipotle-Honey Sauce (recipe follows)
2 tablespoons vegetable oil

1. Line two baking sheets with parchment paper. Combine chicken, eggs, bread crumbs, cilantro, lime juice, garlic, 1 tablespoon adobo sauce and salt in medium bowl; mix well. Shape mixture into 48 meatballs. Place meatballs on prepared baking sheets. Cover with plastic wrap; refrigerate 1 hour.

2. Preheat oven to 400°F. Prepare Chipotle-Honey Sauce.

3. Brush meatballs with oil; bake 12 minutes. Transfer meatballs to baking dish. Add sauce; stir until coated. Bake 10 minutes or until meatballs are heated through and glazed with sauce.   *Makes 4 dozen meatballs*

Chipotle-Honey Sauce

3/4 cup honey
1/3 cup chicken broth
1/3 cup tomato paste
2 to 3 whole chipotle peppers in adobo sauce
1 tablespoon lime juice
2 teaspoons Dijon mustard
1/2 teaspoon salt

Combine all ingredients in food processor or blender; process until smooth.
Makes about 1 1/2 cups

Meatballs with a Twist

Chicken Meatballs with Chipotle-Honey Sauce

Pesto Meatballs with Spaghetti

1 pound ground turkey
⅓ cup plain dry bread crumbs
¼ cup grated Parmesan cheese
¼ cup milk
2 teaspoons dried basil
½ teaspoon garlic powder
½ teaspoon black pepper
1 tablespoon olive oil
1 can (about 14 ounces) stewed tomatoes, undrained
1½ cups chopped mushrooms
1 medium green bell pepper, chopped
½ cup chopped onion
6 cups hot cooked spaghetti

1. Combine turkey, bread crumbs, cheese, milk, basil, garlic powder and black pepper in large bowl; mix well. Shape mixture into 24 meatballs.

2. Heat oil in nonstick skillet over medium-high heat. Brown meatballs in two batches; remove from skillet. Add tomatoes with juice, mushrooms, bell pepper and onion to skillet; simmer 5 to 6 minutes or until softened.

3. Return meatballs to skillet; cook 10 to 15 minutes or until cooked through (165°F).

4. Serve meatballs and sauce over spaghetti.   *Makes 6 servings*

Pesto Meatballs with Spaghetti

Turkey and Veggie Meatballs with Fennel

    1 pound ground turkey
    ½ cup finely chopped green onions
    ½ cup finely chopped green bell pepper
    ⅓ cup oats
    ¼ cup shredded carrots
    ¼ cup grated Parmesan cheese
    2 egg whites, beaten
    2 cloves garlic, minced
    ½ teaspoon dried Italian seasoning
    ¼ teaspoon whole fennel seeds
    ¼ teaspoon salt
    ⅛ teaspoon red pepper flakes (optional)
    1 tablespoon olive oil

1. Combine turkey, green onions, bell pepper, oats, carrots, cheese, egg whites, garlic, Italian seasoning, fennel seeds, salt and red pepper flakes, if desired, in large bowl; mix well. Shape mixture into 36 (1-inch) meatballs.

2. Heat oil in large nonstick skillet over medium-high heat. Add meatballs; cook 11 minutes or until brown on all sides and cooked through (165°F). Serve immediately or cool and freeze.

3. To freeze, place cooled meatballs in 1-gallon resealable freezer food storage bag. Seal and freeze bag flat for easier storage and faster thawing.

4. To thaw, remove desired amount of meatballs from bag and reseal bag, releasing any excess air. Place meatballs on microwavable plate; microwave on HIGH 20 to 30 seconds or until heated through.

Makes 6 servings

Meatballs with a Twist

Turkey and Veggie Meatballs with Fennel

Lemon-Mint Meatballs
with Lemon Orzo

¾ pound ground chicken
2 green onions, minced
2 tablespoons minced fresh mint
2 tablespoons egg substitute
3 cloves garlic, minced
3 teaspoons grated lemon peel, divided
½ teaspoon dried oregano
¼ teaspoon black pepper
3 cups reduced-sodium chicken broth
3 cloves garlic, sliced
1 cup (6 ounces) uncooked orzo pasta
1 tablespoon lemon juice
½ (10-ounce) package spinach leaves, torn

Microwave Directions

1. Spray 11×7-inch microwavable dish with nonstick cooking spray. Combine chicken, green onions, mint, egg substitute, minced garlic, 2 teaspoons lemon peel, oregano and pepper in medium bowl; mix well. Shape mixture into 12 meatballs. Place in prepared baking dish.

2. Combine broth and sliced garlic in large saucepan; bring to a boil over high heat. Stir in orzo. Reduce heat to medium; simmer 8 to 10 minutes or until tender. Reduce heat to low; stir in remaining 1 teaspoon lemon peel and lemon juice. Gradually add spinach; cook and stir until spinach is wilted. Remove from heat; cover to keep warm.

3. Microwave meatballs on HIGH 2 minutes. Rearrange meatballs, moving from outer edges to center of pan. Microwave on HIGH 1 to 2 minutes or until cooked through (165°F).

4. Spoon orzo into shallow bowls or rimmed plates; top with meatballs.
Makes 4 servings

Meatballs with a Twist

Lemon-Mint Meatballs with Lemon Orzo

String Cheese Spaghetti & Meatballs

  1 pound ground beef
½ cup Italian seasoned dry bread crumbs
  1 egg
  1 jar (1 pound 10 ounces) RAGÚ® Organic Pasta Sauce
  1 cup cubed mozzarella cheese (about 4 ounces)
  8 ounces regular or whole wheat spaghetti, cooked and drained

1. In medium bowl, combine ground beef, bread crumbs and egg; shape into 12 meatballs.

2. In 3-quart saucepan, bring Pasta Sauce to a boil over medium-high heat. Gently stir in uncooked meatballs.

3. Reduce heat to low and simmer covered, stirring occasionally, 20 minutes or until meatballs are done. To serve, toss meatballs and sauce with mozzarella cheese and hot spaghetti.　*Makes 4 servings*

Meatball Surprise

  1 pound ground beef
½ box (6.25 ounces) stuffing mix for chicken
  1 can (10¾ ounces) condensed cream of mushroom soup
  1 can (10¾ ounces) condensed cream of celery soup
  2 tablespoons dried onion soup mix
  1 cup milk
  2 cups hot cooked rice

Prepare stuffing according to package directions. Divide ground beef into 8 portions; flatten into thin patties. Spoon prepared stuffing onto middle of patties; roll into balls, sealing ground beef around stuffing. Place meatballs on baking sheet and bake at 350°F until cooked through.

In medium saucepan, combine soups, soup mix and milk. Stir over medium heat until hot. Spoon hot rice onto serving platter; top with meatballs and soup mixture.　*Makes 4 servings*

Favorite recipe from **North Dakota Beef Commission**

Meatballs with a Twist

String Cheese Spaghetti & Meatballs

Turkey Meatballs with Yogurt-Cucumber Sauce

2 tablespoons olive oil, divided
1 cup finely chopped onion
2 cloves garlic, minced
1¼ pounds ground turkey or lamb
½ cup plain dry bread crumbs
¼ cup whipping cream
1 egg, beaten
3 tablespoons chopped fresh mint
1 teaspoon salt
⅛ teaspoon ground red pepper
   Yogurt-Cucumber Sauce (recipe follows)

1. Line two baking sheets with parchment paper. Heat 1 tablespoon oil in medium skillet over medium-high heat. Add onion; cook and stir 3 minutes or until softened. Add garlic; cook and stir 30 seconds. Let cool slightly.

2. Combine turkey, onion mixture, bread crumbs, cream, egg, mint, salt and red pepper in large bowl; mix well. Shape mixture into 40 meatballs. Place on prepared baking sheets. Cover with plastic wrap and refrigerate 1 hour.

3. Meanwhile, prepare Yogurt-Cucumber Sauce. Preheat oven to 400°F. Brush meatballs with remaining 1 tablespoon oil. Bake 15 to 20 minutes, turning once during baking. Serve with sauce.   *Makes 40 meatballs*

Yogurt-Cucumber Sauce

1 container (7 ounces) plain Greek-style yogurt
½ cup peeled, seeded and finely chopped cucumber
2 teaspoons grated lemon peel
2 teaspoons lemon juice
2 teaspoons chopped fresh mint
¼ teaspoon salt

Combine all ingredients in small bowl. Refrigerate until ready to serve.
Makes about 1 cup

Meatballs with a Twist

Turkey Meatballs with Yogurt-Cucumber Sauce

Acknowledgments

The publisher would like to thank the companies and organizations listed below for the use of their recipes and photographs in this publication.

ACH Food Companies, Inc.

American Lamb Board

The Beef Checkoff

BelGioioso® Cheese Inc.

Campbell Soup Company

Cream of Wheat® Cereal

Dole Food Company, Inc.

The Golden Grain Company®

Holland House®

Hormel Foods, LLC

National Pork Board

National Turkey Federation

Nestlé USA

North Dakota Beef Commission

Ortega®, A Division of B&G Foods, Inc.

The Quaker® Oatmeal Kitchens

Reckitt Benckiser LLC.

Recipes courtesy of the Reynolds Kitchens

Unilever

Index

Index

Index

Metric
Conversion Chart

VOLUME
MEASUREMENTS (dry)

1/8 teaspoon = 0.5 mL
1/4 teaspoon = 1 mL
1/2 teaspoon = 2 mL
3/4 teaspoon = 4 mL
1 teaspoon = 5 mL
1 tablespoon = 15 mL
2 tablespoons = 30 mL
1/4 cup = 60 mL
1/3 cup = 75 mL
1/2 cup = 125 mL
2/3 cup = 150 mL
3/4 cup = 175 mL
1 cup = 250 mL
2 cups = 1 pint = 500 mL
3 cups = 750 mL
4 cups = 1 quart = 1 L

VOLUME MEASUREMENTS (fluid)

1 fluid ounce (2 tablespoons) = 30 mL
4 fluid ounces (1/2 cup) = 125 mL
8 fluid ounces (1 cup) = 250 mL
12 fluid ounces (1 1/2 cups) = 375 mL
16 fluid ounces (2 cups) = 500 mL

WEIGHTS (mass)

1/2 ounce = 15 g
1 ounce = 30 g
3 ounces = 90 g
4 ounces = 120 g
8 ounces = 225 g
10 ounces = 285 g
12 ounces = 360 g
16 ounces = 1 pound = 450 g

DIMENSIONS

1/16 inch = 2 mm
1/8 inch = 3 mm
1/4 inch = 6 mm
1/2 inch = 1.5 cm
3/4 inch = 2 cm
1 inch = 2.5 cm

OVEN
TEMPERATURES

250°F = 120°C
275°F = 140°C
300°F = 150°C
325°F = 160°C
350°F = 180°C
375°F = 190°C
400°F = 200°C
425°F = 220°C
450°F = 230°C

BAKING PAN SIZES

Utensil	Size in Inches/Quarts	Metric Volume	Size in Centimeters
Baking or Cake Pan (square or rectangular)	8×8×2	2 L	20×20×5
	9×9×2	2.5 L	23×23×5
	12×8×2	3 L	30×20×5
	13×9×2	3.5 L	33×23×5
Loaf Pan	8×4×3	1.5 L	20×10×7
	9×5×3	2 L	23×13×7
Round Layer Cake Pan	8×1½	1.2 L	20×4
	9×1½	1.5 L	23×4
Pie Plate	8×1¼	750 mL	20×3
	9×1¼	1 L	23×3
Baking Dish or Casserole	1 quart	1 L	—
	1½ quart	1.5 L	—
	2 quart	2 L	—